Writing Center Perspectives

edited by

Byron L. Stay
Mount St. Mary's College

Christina Murphy
Texas Christian University

Eric H. Hobson
St. Louis College of Pharmacy

NWCA Press
1995

Writing Center Perspectives

Copyright © 1995 NWCA Press

Published 1995 by NWCA Press

PO Box 7007
16300 Old Emmitsburg Road
Emmitsburg, Maryland 21727

ISBN 0-9648067-0-3

About the Editors

Byron L. Stay, President of the National Writing Centers Association, is Associate Professor of Rhetoric and Writing and Associate Dean at Mount St. Mary's College. He serves on the editorial boards of *The Writing Center Journal* and *Dialogue*, and his articles have appeared in *Composition Studies, Writing Center Journal, Journal of Teaching Writing, Composition Chronicle, Writing Lab Newsletter*, and in numerous anthologies of composition instruction.

Christina Murphy is the Director of the William L. Adams Writing Center and the Co-director of the University Writing Program at Texas Christian University. She is the First Vice-President of the National Writing Centers Association and will assume the Presidency of the NWCA in 1996. Her essays on writing centers, rhetorical theory, and psychoanalytic theory have appeared in a wide range of composition and psychoanalytic journals as well as in several collections. With Steve Sherwood she co-authored *The St. Martin's Sourcebook for Writing Tutors* and with Joe Law co-edited *Landmark Essays on Writing Centers* for Hermagoras Press. Her essay, "The Writing Center and Social Constructionist Theory," won the Outstanding Scholarship Award for 1994 from NWCA.

Eric H. Hobson coordinates the writing programs and is director of the St. Louis College of Pharmacy Writing Center where he is working to develop a writing-center-based writing-across-the-curriculum program to meet the needs of a professional school. The co-author of *Reading and Writing in High Schools: A Whole Language Approach*, his book *Where Theory and Practice Collide: The Writing Center* is forthcoming. In addition to publishing widely in writing center and composition journals, he serves on the Executive Board of the National Writing Centers Association.

Introduction

The idea for this collection of essays emerged from the First National Writing Centers Conference in New Orleans, Louisiana, in 1994. The conference provided a forum for writing center concerns, and the presentations proved so rich in insights that the Steering Committee members who had coordinated the conference decided that selected papers should be brought together and made into a book for the enrichment of writing center personnel everywhere. Eventually, as the volume developed, papers from a number of regional conferences were also included as well as several essays invited by the editors. The editors wish to thank the other Steering Committee members—Ray Wallace, Joan A. Mullin, and Jim McDonald—for helping to make the conference and this volume significant contributions to the writing center field.

This volume is also historically significant as the first book to be published by the NWCA Press, which was founded in 1995 as an outlet for writing center scholarship. The editors inaugurate NWCA Press with this collection of essays that highlights the diversity of the writing center discipline and records important innovative approaches to defining writing center work within the academy as we approach the twenty-first century and its educational and ideological challenges.

Dave Healy opens the collection with the essay, "In the Temple of the Familiar: The Writing Center as Church," in which he proposes the church as a historically valuable analog for many of the complex issues within the discipline. Too many theorists, Healy claims, discuss writing centers as if ideology were the determining factor in shaping the "multidimensionality of identity and affiliation" when, in fact, "like churches, writing centers develop particular styles, strategies, and missions based on many influences, the majority of which are more situational and demographic than ideological." Consequently, as Healy argues, "perhaps the sociology of religion can be instructive for us as we look more closely at the circumstantial forces that shape writing centers."

Healy's emphasis on the "situational and demographic" forces that shape writing centers and their missions is found in the essays in this volume that describe the accomplishments of individual programs. In "Writing Centers and Writing Assessment: A Discipline-Based Approach," Mark L. Waldo, Jacob Blumner, and Mary Webb describe a new approach to writing assessment and writing across the curriculum at the University of Nevada. The program "is essentially discipline based, meaning that the goals, purposes, and forms for writing are discovered in the disciplines themselves, not translated or imposed from one discipline to another."

The writing center's role in responding to the requirements of disciplines across the curriculum and to the needs of a particular campus are discussed in detail along with the challenges of responsive innovation. In "E Pluribus Unum: An Administrator Rounds Up Mavericks and Money," David E. Schwalm describes the establishment of the writing center and the writing program at Arizona State University West as non-traditional ventures on a non-traditional campus not bound by conventional hierarchies or the general distribution of programs and disciplinary boundaries found on most campuses. Joseph Saling in "Centering: What Writing Centers Need to Do" describes the writing center's role at Massachusetts Bay Community College in addressing the needs of students participating in a joint program between universities and area community colleges. Saling's focus is upon the writing center's contributions to the students' development and also to retention.

Albert C. DeCiccio, Michael J. Rossi, and Kathleen Shine Cain address the tensions between the ideological demands placed upon the writing center and the practical realities of everyday operations. In "Walking the Tightrope: Negotiating Between the Ideal and the Practical in the Writing Center," they state that "while writing center theorists debate with one another, a parallel conversation among tutors and tutees is constructing real theory." Jeanne Simpson carries this same point of view into a discussion of how writing centers are perceived by administrators. In "Perceptions, Realities, and Possibilities: Central Administration and Writing Centers," Simpson contends that many of the common perceptions of central administration by writing center personnel are actually misperceptions of power structures within the academy. In reality, "accreditation, accountability (assessment), staffing plans, space allocation, and personnel dollars" are "the nuts-and-bolts concerns, the daily assignment of administration. It is crucial [for writing center personnel] to understand that." Thus, as Simpson claims, "a writing center for Central Administration is space, student use, personnel dollars, productivity, and a program that requires assessment and evaluation on the basis of institutional mission and priorities." Joe Law addresses the issue of how "institutional mission and priorities" affect administrative decisions concerning writing centers in "Accreditation and the Writing Center: A Proposal for Action." In discussing how writing centers must continually defend their roles and fight for their existence within the academy, Law calls for a national accreditation of writing centers—similar to the regional accreditation of colleges and universities—that would define specific criteria for evaluating the accomplishments of individual writing centers. The benefits of such an approach would be many, as Law indicates: "A writing center's funding depends upon how its effectiveness is perceived; likewise, writing center staff wanting increased recognition as professionals gain that respect according to the way they are perceived. Clearly, then, evaluating and presenting oneself and one's program are crucial activities. Unfortunately, many writing centers are still perceived as ancillary to 'real' instruction and the writing center staff regarded as second- or third-class members of the academy." A program of national accreditation would help to overcome this deficiency and to lend credence to a writing center's accomplishments on its own campus and within the discipline as a whole.

Steve Sherwood in "The Dark Side of the Helping Personality: Student Dependency and the Potential for Tutor Burnout" and Wangeci JoAnne Karuri in "Must We Always Grin and Bear It?" consider how the emotional aspects of tutoring can negatively affect tutors. Sherwood focuses on the underside of altruism when he states, "We're quite right to take pride in working hard to help students, but we should be careful not to fall prey to our own good intentions. For when altruism degrades into neurotic unselfishness, it can lead to student dependency and tutor burnout. It can also lead those we serve (our students, colleagues, and administrators) to take our services for granted." Karuri discusses the emotional toll for tutors when they must respond to student papers "with offensive content or ideology." She reflects upon this issue in these terms: "Since the writing center's goal is to help writers effectively present ideas, should we simply ignore the disturbing or repulsive elements in these texts? How do we reconcile our professional duties to student writers with our need to defend personal beliefs and values?" Through discussions of several tutorials and through the presentation of survey results from the national conference, Karuri offers practical suggestions on how tutors addressing objectionable papers and topics can avoid "unproductive" conferences and fulfill their responsibilities while still being faithful to their own philosophies and personal values.

A number of writers in this collection seek to define the tutor's role and to examine the metaphors that have guided theoretical discussions of the tutoring process. Donna Fontanarose Rabuck examines the tutor's role as an ally and partner in the writing process in "Giving Birth to Voice: The Professional Writing Tutor as Midwife." She contends that the midwife analogy aptly describes the tutor's relationship to the student in the writing-as-process paradigm. The tutor's role is not to be directive but to be assistive, much in the way a midwife facilitates a birth but does not control the event. In a similar fashion, the effective tutor lends his or her expertise to the writer's efforts to create, but always does so in a collaborative role in which the responsibility for and the ultimate achievement of the writing remains with the student. Jane Cogie emphasizes a similar non-directive approach in "Resisting the Editorial Urge in Writing Center Conferences: An Essential Focus in Tutor Training." As she states, "To help student writers genuinely improve, tutors need more than good intentions and more than a thorough versing in the qualities of good writing or tutoring techniques and theory .... Helping tutors find strategies for assisting student writers is not enough. Tutors must also be sensitized to recognize when their focus has shifted away from the student."

Collaborative effort is also the central theme of Dawn M. Formo's and Jennifer Welsh's "Tickling the Student's Ear: Collaboration and the Teacher/Student Relationship." Formo and Welsh assert that "the one-on-one conference between teacher and student is one of the most common tools used in collaborative teaching. While this type of collaboration has the potential to be a truly equal partnership in working on a paper, it is also the point at which both parties must negotiate the precarious boundary between the two levels of power established by the academic institution." Negotiating this "precarious boundary" is also addressed by Carmen Werder and Roberta R. Buck in "Assessing Writing Conference Talk: An Ethnographic Method." The authors offer a method for assessing the efficacy of tutorials by focusing on the types of questions tutors raise with students and the critical thinking skills tutors encourage in the process. Cheryl Reed draws from industrial psychology theories to discuss issues of empowerment in student-centered pedagogies. Her thesis is that "both sets of theories address the process of constructing a subjectivity that is legible and that carries weight within the discursive system in which one functions. However we configure the student/instructor relationship—as mentorship, as collaboration, as empowerment—it is an integral part of a hierarchical network of task-oriented agents carrying on the 'enterprise' of the university."

Explorations of the writing center's potential as a research site and also as an "alternative space" for new techno-pedagogies complement investigations of the writing center's traditional role within the academy. Julie Hagemann in "Writing Centers as Sites for Writing Transfer Research" explores "the ways undergraduates transfer skills from one course to another" and what role the writing center can play. She presents the results of her analysis of Lih Mei's tutorial sessions over an academic semester in reference to numerous assignments and issues in her courses and uses her conclusions to affirm the writing center's potential role in knowledge transfer. Robert W. Holderer in "Holistic Scoring: A Valuable Tool for Improving Writing Across the Curriculum" and Jean Kiedaisch and Sue Dinitz in "Using Collaborative Groups to Teach Critical Thinking" emphasize new opportunities for the writing center to shape writing across the curriculum programs by focusing on critical thinking skills. Cynthia Haynes-Burton brings the metaphors and concepts of cyberspace to bear in her analysis of "Intellectual (Proper)ty in Writing Centers: Retro

Texts and Positive Plagiarism." She contends that the writing center, with its emphasis upon collaboration and its challenges to the hegemony of the traditional concept of the solitary author within the academy, offers an exceptional site and opportunity for testing the limits of what constitute both intellectual property and plagiarism in postmodern society. According to Haynes-Burton, "we are living in the time zone of amazing promises ..., moving toward technographic redefinitions of literacy, composition, and collaboration at speeds in which writing is currency in the net." As a result,

> The writing center ... has consistently wrestled with the issue of "intellectual property." Unfortunately, writing centers battle a classic double bind: either we are perceived as helping students too much, or not enough. So, we fly low, avoiding the academic radar designed to fix our location and bring us back to base, and back in line. Recent technology allows us to construct new terrains like online writing centers (OWLs) and new communities like text-based multi-user domains (MOOs). Tutors and students traffic uneasily in the stealth landscape between collaboration and appropriation, a region of textual shadows and mis-located meanings, a region of surveillance and the surveilled student subject. Granted, it is not popular to use military metaphors, much less to signal an assault, but to analyze a fortress sometimes you have to tear it down, to dismantle its political and economic walls.

Haynes-Burton's essay returns us to the central questions of the volume: how shall writing centers be conceptualized, configured, reconfigured—dismantled, if you will—to respond to the demands of individual campuses, the academy, social systems, and ultimately of the sociocultural and historical eras that writing centers participate in defining? As this volume indicates, there is no monolithic definition of *the* writing center; instead, there is only a myriad of innovative responses to the ways in which writing centers can contribute to the educational and ideological issues of our day. The many voices, experiences, and approaches detailed in this collection attest to the vibrancy of writing centers in postmodern times. *Writing Center Perspectives* is a testament to the complexities of the challenges writing centers face and a signal that "walking the tightrope" between "the ideal and the real" in the writing center field will continue as one of the most meaningful educational challenges and opportunities of our time.

—Byron L. Stay
—Christina Murphy
—Eric H. Hobson

Table of Contents

In the Temple of the Familiar: The Writing Center as Church

Dave Healy
University of Minnesota

Metaphor making proliferates in conditions of indeterminacy. We know what flowers are; hence, a rose is a rose is a rose. But because we're not quite sure what love is, to describe it we compare love to things we do know, e.g., a red, red rose that's newly sprung in June. Writing centers, because of their historically indeterminate status in the academy, have prompted a good deal of metaphor making. Because we have often been in the position of attempting to define ourselves to ignorant or misguided colleagues, we cast about for fruitful comparisons. "Well, you see, writing centers are like ... labs ... or clinics ... or birthing rooms, or ... studios, or .... And those of us who work in writing centers are like ... doctors ... or therapists ... or midwives ... or coaches ... or consultants, or ..."

Of course, any comparison is limited and incomplete. Also, writing centers, both individually and collectively, continue to evolve. For these reasons, our metaphors are subject to continual critique and revision. Peter Carino, for example, traces the evolution of metaphors from clinic to lab to center ("What"), and Richard Leahy explores the contemporary resonance of "centeredness" and "centrism." While Carino and Leahy look at self-styled comparisons—i.e., how writing center personnel have represented themselves to the rest of the world—Michael Pemberton is interested in debunking metaphors that outsiders have imposed on us: the writing center as prison, hospital, or madhouse. Thomas Hemmeter, on the other hand, takes up a comparison that we have quite willingly perpetuated—the writing center and the classroom—and argues that our dualistic discourse has the effect of depicting the center as inferior or incomplete.

These analysts differ not only in the comparisons they consider, but also in their conceptions of metaphoricity. For Hemmeter, we *are* the metaphors we make: "The writing center *is* our words, a linguistic phenomenon" (44). Pemberton, on the other hand, sees the metaphorical as different from the actual. Metaphorical constructs, he says, "conceive of writing centers not directly, in terms of what they actually *are*, but associatively, in terms of what they seem to resemble" (11). For his part, Carino sees writing centers as both social and linguistic phenomena, "social in the sense of the praxis that goes on there, linguistic in the sense that all of that praxis is mediated by language both as it occurs and in any attempts we make to document it" (32).

Though these theorists differ in their analyses and their conclusions, they share the conviction that metaphor is a powerful and revealing means of representation. As Lakoff and Johnson argue, metaphors are not mere ornament or rhetorical flourish; instead, metaphor is a fundamental part of our very way of conceptualizing. Metaphors, from this perspective, are not only ubiquitous, but inevitable. Because we have grown accustomed to the term "writing center," we tend not to realize that the very name we go by is a metaphor. Sometimes it takes a Peter Carino or a Richard Leahy to remind us of the metaphoricity of "centrism."

I, too, take metaphors and metaphor making seriously, and like the observers cited above, I believe that the metaphors we invent for writing centers reveal a great deal about ourselves—our attitudes toward the places we work and the people we work with. In that spirit, I would like to spin out some implications of a little-used metaphor: the writing center as church. I find this comparison useful primarily in its illumination of the range of beliefs and practices that characterize writing centers. Though we sometimes speak of the Church with a capital C, almost any discussion of American religious institutions must fairly quickly acknowledge our religious pluralism. Yet despite our diversity, the term "church" continues to have some common resonance in the culture at large. Similarly, though we sometimes talk about "the idea of a writing center," as if there were a Platonic form we could all recognize and delineate, most discussions of writing centers eventually descend to the particular—or at least they should.

Steve North is a case in point. When North felt obliged to revisit his influential "The Idea of a Writing Center" eleven years after its publication, his attempt to clarify and re-envision his original Idea led to a description of changes at a particular institution—his own, SUNY–Albany—involving a particular writing program and writing center. In responding to a letter to the editor of *The Writing Center Journal*, North describes the amended idea of a writing center presented in "Revisiting" as a result of

> more than fifteen years of negotiating that included, among lots of other things ..., the founding of the Writing Center, the phasing out of freshman composition (as we knew it), the development of a university-wide writing-across-the-curriculum (WAC) program, the emergence of the Writing Center as the hub for all WAC activity, the establishment ... of a Center for Excellence in Teaching and Learning—all of which, one way or another, have been aimed at altering the role writing plays at the University at Albany. ("Letters" 184)

This tension between the general and the particular, between The Idea of a Writing Center and the practices of actual writing centers, has not been sufficiently acknowledged and analyzed within our profession. Though we readily concede that writing centers have evolved, we tend, as Carino notes, to view that process diachronically ("Early"). The result is an unexamined assumption that, while today's writing centers are different from yesterday's writing labs, contemporary centers are fairly similar to each other. Perhaps we would be less likely to make such an assumption if we conceived of writing centers as churches.

American religious history is the history of denominationalism. As Richard Niebuhr has shown, denominations tend to form along political, regional, and socioeconomic lines as well as theological or ideological ones. Though a denomination's leaders may have often "transcended class and economic conditions to set forth a purely religious ideal with divine disregard for mundane interests in caste or in financial security," yet, says Niebuhr, "the acceptance of their ideals by a particular group, and the modification of the religious doctrine by selective emphasis has often been due to other than purely religious motives" (78-79). Though Niebuhr laments the "proneness toward compromise which characterizes the whole history of the church" (3), the fact remains that people's material conditions will influence their religious beliefs and practices. Thus, it is possible to argue, à la Nietzsche, that Christianity is the religion of slaves, or to agree with Weber that it has always been essentially a bourgeois religion.

The relationship between the general and the particular, between ideology and practice, has concerned writing center theorists as well as religious historians. Thinking about writing centers as churches can provide a helpful perspective on the troubling question of what the relationship should be between writing center theory and praxis. One lesson from Niebuhr's analysis of denominationalism is that it may be misleading to assume that praxis follows from theory. What people do is influenced by a host of things, ideology being only one of those. The result of this dynamic in both the religious and academic spheres is that theoretical justification often comes *after* a particular practice has proven itself convenient or effective.

For example, a church that promulgates a particular model for male-female relationships and family life may well have arrived at its position for reasons more sociological or political than theological. The general educational level of a congregation, its situatedness (e.g., rural vs. urban), the individual family histories that parishioners bring to congregational life—these and other factors will predispose a local group to exhibit certain attitudes and behaviors. The attempt to find theological justification for its beliefs and practices by, say, biblical exegesis, may turn out to be *ex post facto.* Similarly, a writing center might develop effective strategies for working with its unique clientele and then later look for ways to account for and support its praxis theoretically. That, in fact, is how the whole peer tutoring initiative of the 1970s developed, according to Kenneth Bruffee. Peer tutoring was, in part, a response to the demands created by open admissions and the failure of traditional, professionally staffed support programs to engage the students most in need of those programs. Conceived of as an alternative to, rather than an extension of, the traditional classroom, peer tutoring "made learning a two-way street, since students' work tended to improve when they got help from peer tutors and tutors learned from the students they helped and from the activity of tutoring itself" (4). It was only later, says Bruffee, that practitioners began learning that "much of this practical experience and the insights it yielded have a conceptual rationale, a theoretical dimension, that had escaped us earlier as we muddled through, trying to solve practical problems in practical ways" (4).

Like churches, writing centers exist in varied institutional and political contexts. Should we expect a writing center in a large, racially and ethnically diverse university to operate the same as one at a small, relatively homogenous private college? Should a center that serves primarily first-generation college students, refugees, and returning adults look like one whose 18-22-year-old clients graduated from affluent suburban high schools? Should a writing center housed in the English Department function similarly to one operating out of Student Services? These are difficult questions, and it is not my purpose here to answer them. I raise them, instead, to illustrate a three-fold point: (1) We have not spent much time addressing such questions; (2) The attempt to grapple with such questions would be aided by considering other institutions that face similar issues; (3) The church is such an institution.

Writing center analysts who consider the relationship between theory and praxis tend to do so without factoring in the obvious situational differences facing writing centers. Eric Hobson—in "Writing Center Practice Often Counters Its Theory. So What?"—argues that "no single theory can dictate writing center instruction. Instead, we must reshape theory to fit our particular needs in the particular historically located situations in which writing center practitioners find themselves" (8). Yet Hobson has nothing specific to say about those particular needs or situations.

Andrea Lunsford distinguishes among three kinds of writing centers: the Storehouse, the Garret, and the Burkean Parlor. But while Lunsford acknowledges the existence of different centers with different philosophies and practices, she attributes those differences solely to competing *theories*. The Storehouse Center, which "operates as information stations or storehouses, prescribing and handing out skills and strategies to individual learners," does so, says Lunsford, because of its view of knowledge as "exterior," "directly accessible," and "individually derived and held" (4). Garret Centers, on the other hand, "are informed by a deep-seated belief in individual 'genius,' in the Romantic sense of the term " and "a deep-seated attachment to the American brand of individualism" (4-5). Garret Centers see knowledge as "interior, as inside the student, and the writing center's job as helping students get in touch with this knowledge, as a way to find their unique voices, their individual and unique powers" (5). In Lunsford's scheme, both Storehouse and Garret Centers are inferior to what she calls Burkean Parlor Centers, which are based on "the notion of knowledge as always contextually bound, as always socially constructed" (8). Nowhere in Lunsford's analysis, though, is there any indication that variety among writing centers might result from anything other than theoretical differences. Not only does she assume that practice always follows from theory, but she ignores the potential influence on practice of anything *but* theory.

Unlike writing center theorists, theologians have devoted considerable attention to the relationships among belief, situational context, and practice. I have already noted Niebuhr's emphasis on sociological and demographic influences in the development of denominations. The most widely studied of such influences have been economic ones. Max Weber's *The Protestant Ethic and the Spirit of Capitalism* set the stage for many subsequent analyses. Weber posited an "elective affinity" between certain religious beliefs—e.g., predestination, work as divine calling—and the ethics of daily work life. The result of this affinity was a flourishing of entrepreneurial capitalism within Protestant Europe. There have been numerous attempts to test the validity of Weber's thesis for American religion. One notable study is Laserwitz's, which found that education, occupation, and income data sorted out into a social hierarchy, with Episcopalians, Jews, and Presbyterians at the top; Methodists, Lutherans, and Roman Catholics in the middle; and Baptists at the bottom.

Other sociologists have focused on different variables, such as geography and ethnicity. Gibson Winter's *The Suburban Captivity of the Churches* addresses the troubling question of why Protestantism has had "notable success in the growing suburbs, [but has] suffered dismal failures in the central areas of the metropolis" (15). Winter attempts to account for the varied factors affecting the religious identity of urbanites. He notes, for example, that in ethnic churches, religious life "became a counterforce to the upward mobility and Americanization of immigrant children. Parents and pastors clung to an ethnic style of religion as a protest against the break-up of the ethnic community of identity" (131). Harvey Cox tries to articulate a "theology of social change" for what he calls "the secular city." According to Cox, "In our day the secular metropolis stands as both the pattern of our life together and the symbol of our view of the world" (1). Cox's book is an attempt re-envision the mission of the church in a secularized, urbanized age.

What is notable about these sociologists of religion is their recognition of the multidimensionality of religious identity and affiliation. People associate with particular churches for many reasons, and churches develop particular styles, strategies, and missions based on many influences, the majority of which are more situational and demographic than ideological. Certainly, the same is true of writing centers, but our profession has been less forthcoming about acknowledging those influences. Perhaps the sociology of religion can be instructive for us as we look more closely at the circumstantial forces that shape writing centers.

In addition to glossing over our demographic differences, writing center analysts tend to ignore other significant variety among centers. Among the many ways that writing centers differ, perhaps none is more consequential than the makeup of their staff. Much theoretical justification for writing centers has appealed to Bruffee; consequently, much of the writing center literature implicitly assumes a peer tutoring model. The fact is, however, that some writing centers operate with "professional" (i.e., degree-bearing) staff, and at some institutions graduate students serve both as classroom teachers and writing center tutors. This difference is not trivial. Issues of authority, ethos, and conference dynamics are significantly affected by the perceived status of a center's employees. Once again, the range of practices in place at different writing centers might be better understood by looking at other institutions that face similar issues, and once again the church proves to be an appropriate and helpful comparison.

The status of its principal employee, the minister, has been problematic for the church at least since the Reformation. A central tenet of the Reformation was the priesthood of *all* believers. But if all are priests, if all are called to minister, then in what meaningful sense can one talk about the clergy? As Protestant church historian James Logan observes, "We have not yet in reflection or practice resolved the issue left us by the Reformation of the relationship between clergy and laity who possess a common baptism into a ministry of reconciliation and yet perform an extraordinary ordination of the clergy 'set apart' ministry" (8). Most attempts to resolve the issue, to justify the existence of the clergy as an office, have emphasized the clergy's role in ministering, not to society at large—which is everyone's job—but to the church. In this connection, St. Paul's counsel to the Ephesians is often cited as support for a clerical office: "And his gifts were that some should be apostles, some prophets, some evangelists, some pastors and teachers, for the equipment of the

saints, for the work of the ministry, for building up the body of Christ"
(Eph. 4:11-12, RSV).

Hendrik Kraemer argues, however, that the Greek text gives no
support for a comma after the word "saints" and goes on to observe that
repunctuating the passage gives it a different slant altogether:

> It is really startling to notice how radically the meaning of the
> text is altered by the removal of this comma. It restores to the text
> the meaning which fits in with the picture the New Testament
> gives of *all* the saints, i.e. all the members, being ministers,
> servants to the upbuilding of the Church. It rules out the use of
> the text as a corroboration for the condition of the Church as we
> know it by tradition, viz. the "ministry," the diakonia as a
> specialized sphere. Of this specialized sphere the Church in its
> primitive, fluid state was scarcely conscious. (140)

Albert Sauls presents a similar position, pointing out that the New
Testament word for "ministry," *diakonia*, means literally "waiting on
tables" (Luke 17:8) and came to mean "one who serves others." In this
sense, every participant in the early Church was expected to be a minister
(85).

In its most basic and dramatic form, then, the debate concerning the
ministerial calling crystallizes in two competing images: in James Dittes'
words, the "expert" vs. the "fellow pilgrim." Is the minister somehow "set
apart," or is he a "man among men"?[1] Though this terminology is of recent
origin, the debate is not. Mark Ellingsen sees its roots in the writings of
Martin Luther. The terminology Ellingsen adopts is "authoritarian leader"
vs. "facilitator." By exercising authority, the minister emphasizes his set-
apart status: he is over and above the congregation. As a facilitator, on the
other hand, the pastor attempts to implement shared congregational
leadership and thus emphasizes his status as a fellow pilgrim. Ellingsen
argues that these "two lines of thought about the ordained ministry
coexist in tension in Luther's writings" (339). Furthermore, the set-apart
vs. fellow-pilgrim issue has significant implications for the question of
ministerial authority:

> It is in answer to this question [i.e., the question of authority]
> that the two lines of thought in Luther's concept of the ordained
> ministry have been identified. One finds him speaking in some
> places of the authority of the ordained ministry as derived from
> the universal priesthood. Carried to its logical conclusion this
> view of the ministry's authority derived "from below" implies
> the model of minister as facilitator of the congregation .... Yet

one also finds the Reformer speaking of the office as divinely instituted, its authority derived "from above." This line of thought distinguishes pastor and laity and implies that the pastor is in charge. (340-41)

If Luther evidenced some balance between set-apart and fellow-pilgrim conceptions of the clergy, Calvin strongly emphasized the former. During the nineteenth century, however, Calvinist theology was challenged by a more liberal and humanistic religion (Douglas). One influential spokesman for the liberal theology of that day was Henry Ward Beecher, a younger contemporary of Emerson and Thoreau and pastor of the wealthy Plymouth Church in Brooklyn. In "Sphere of the Christian Minister," Beecher provides an eloquent testimonial for the fellow-pilgrim conception of the clergy.

Beecher rejects that conception of the "clerical profession" which holds that "there is a body of men taken up by God's appointment, and set apart from human life, and endowed with special prerogatives, and given special virtues; and that as a class, they stand above their fellow men in authority in moral things" (156). The problem with assigning clergy to a special class, says Beecher, is that "the great body of an aristocracy will work for an aristocracy. The great body of a special class in politics will work for their class; and a body of clergymen will work for themselves" (157). Against the view of the clergy as a special class Beecher opposes one that sees the minister as "a man among men":

> He is not endowed with any gifts beside those which belong to any other men of his mark or make .... No special grace passes over into him, either by the touch of priestly hands, or through any long channel derived from the apostles. He is what he is by the grace of God in the ordinance of his birth, and in the process of his education—just that .... He is just like another man. Call up a layman that is his equal in intelligence, that is his equal in moral power, with his simplicity, sincerity, and directness, and that layman is just as much as he is. There is nothing in ordination; there is nothing in the imposition of hands. God's ordination lies in birth. That is the grand ordination. (157-58)

But Beecher's impassioned apology for a fellow-pilgrim notion of the minister notwithstanding, many people have seen and continue to see the clergyman as set apart. Indeed, as Dittes observes,

> Clergymen are subject to a number of social influences to make them feel "set aside" quite as much as "set apart." Folklore

still commonly supposes a minister to be excluded from such human characteristics as concern for money, anger, sexual temptation, political opinions, family spats, etc.; society institutionalizes the exclusion in such forms as the 4-D draft deferments and the 10 percent store discounts, and the inevitable rituals of alarm when a minister appears in a divorce court or a mental hospital. From his first announcement of his vocational plans as a boy, he has experienced such forms of social exclusion and isolation, both from adults and from his peers. (43)

Many clergy themselves, while they may decry the exclusion and isolation their set-apart status imposes and may at times identify with the mid-nineteenth-century cleric Orville Dewey, who "felt that as a minister he was 'not fairly thrown into the field of life ... [but rather] hedged around with artificial barriers ... a sort of moral eunuch" (qtd. in Douglas 23), nevertheless at other times may see themselves as different, and therefore to some extent necessarily removed, from their parishioners and may find thus themselves identifying with John Updike's middle-aged minister Tom Marshfield:

We stand, brethren, where we stand, in our impossible and often mischievously idle jobs, on a boundary of opposing urgencies where there is often not space enough to set one's feet—we so stand as steeples stand, as emblems; it is our station to be visible and to provide men with the opportunity to profess the impossible that makes their lives possible. The Catholic church in this at least was right; a priest is more than a man, and though the man disintegrate within his vestments, and become degraded beyond the laxest of his flock, the priest can continue to perform his functions, as a scarecrow performs his. (248-49)

Questions the church has debated regarding ministers—whether they should be seen as leaders or facilitators, whether their authority derives from "above" or "below," whether it is the "man" or the "office" that is more important—are instructive for writing center personnel, who have worried a good deal about similar issues. Centers that employ peer tutors might argue, in the spirit of Henry Ward Beecher, that the tutor is endowed with no unusual gifts or special grace, that all writers confront common challenges, and that the service ethic of the writing center is compromised by creating a special class that sees itself as fundamentally different from those it serves. On the other hand, a writing center theorist such as John Trimbur might question whether "peer tutor" is a contradiction in terms and might note, in the spirit of James Dittes, that regardless of how writing center personnel see themselves, they will be perceived as different—removed from the compositional sins that doth so easily beset their less elevated counterparts:

> The tutors' success as undergraduates and their strengths as writers single them out and accentuate the differences between them and their tutees—thereby, in effect, undercutting the peer relationship. Appointment to tutor, after all, invests a certain institutional authority in the tutors that their tutees have not earned. (23)

Trimbur's invocation of institutional authority in the writing center underscores another corollary with clergy. Ellingsen noted that the minister's authority has been seen as deriving both from above and below. From whence comes the tutor's authority—from institutional sanction, or from kindred spirithood with the center's constituency? Trimbur also observes that authority conferred from above is often ambivalent. On the one hand, tutors are those who have mastered and been rewarded by the system; on the other hand, for many traditionalists within the academy, "peer tutoring looks like a case of the 'blind leading the blind'" (22).

Questions about the role and image of tutors feed into the larger issue of the role and image of the writing center itself. What sort of place should the writing center be? What should be its relationship to the larger institution of which it is a part? Terrance Riley worries that the professionalization of writing centers marks an unavoidable compromise of our true calling: "As we professionalize, less and less are we able to assert that our philosophy is liberatory and contrarian .... Each conventionally-measured advance in our professional status, every move closer to the mainstream, reduces our variety and our breadth of vision" (29-30).

Such issues have troubled church leaders as well. How the church as an institution persists over time, how it undergoes what Weber called the "routinization of charisma"—the inevitable process of stabilizing and institutionalizing its original ideals and preparing itself for the demise of its founders—these are matters that have vigorously engaged church historians and sociologists of religion. The most influential formulation regarding the evolution of religious groups has been Ernst Troeltsch's sect-church hypothesis. For Troeltsch the sect is characterized by voluntary membership (conversion), close interpersonal fellowship among members, an "indifferent, tolerant or hostile" attitude toward the world, and an identification with lower-class society. The church, on the other hand, is marked by inherited membership, hierarchical relations, a mission to change the world, and upper-class involvement. Groups tend to evolve from the more sect-like to the more church-like. In the process, they become more accepting of the status quo, seeking to influence the secular order "slowly though a process of adaptation and compromise, a two-way process calling for changes in both the church-like congregation and the secular order" (Winter 115).

It is precisely this kind of development—an accommodation to the status quo and a stratifying of relationships—that Terrance Riley fears for writing centers. Riley traces the evolution of three disciplines in the academy— American literature, literary theory, and composition—and concludes that all three sacrificed much of their earlier strengths for "a professionalization irrelevant to their ends, and often at odds with their expressed ideals" (28). For Riley, applying the sect-to-church hypothesis to the academy would confirm trends that he sees evident there—toward professionalization, bureaucratization, self-protection, and conservatism. But, despite the explanatory power of the sect-church hypothesis, it does not account for all religious groups. Some—e.g., Amish, Plymouth Brethren, Mennonites, Hutterites—have maintained a sect-like presence over a comparatively long period of time. So for those who share Riley's fears about writing centers, there is precedent in the religious sphere for a resistance to accommodation.

One reason writing centers and churches have much in common institutionally is the similar status of their practitioners with respect to the organizations they work within. Although the clergy is a "service profession," it differs from many other such professions in that the clergy's role exists only in reference to the institution it serves. Unlike the physician or lawyer, who sustain rather than are sustained by the organizations they belong to, the minister, as a representative "organization man," is sustained by the organization and has no professional existence apart from it (Galbraith 107-08). As Thomas Gannon has observed, "[W]ithout ecclesiastical (i.e., organizationally imposed) ordination or appointment by the church, clergymen as such have no legitimation—indeed they have no job .... Thus, the context and significance of the clerical profession is the church and not, as with other professions, *society-at-large*" (72-73, emphasis in original). Once ordained, ministers and priests may retain their title ("Reverend" or "Father") apart from any continuing relationship with the organization (i.e., church), but in any practical sense they cease to be considered clergy if they are not associated with some organization.

Writing center personnel, too, like other academics, require institutional affiliation. Though professional editing services exist apart from academic institutions, it is difficult to imagine most writing centers divorced from their institutional context. A recent discussion on WCENTER, a computer list for writing center personnel, found participants responding to an inquiry from someone interested in starting a for-profit online writing center unaffiliated with any college or university. The skepticism that met this proposal reflected a certain amount of defensiveness and turf protection from the academics on the list, but respondents also raised some pertinent questions that underscored the difficulty an independent writing center would face.

Like clergy, writing center personnel live and move and have their being within institutions on which they are dependent for their professional identity. Most other professionals have more mobility. Physicians, for example, usually need some kind of affiliation with a hospital, but if a general practitioner wants to hang out her shingle or start a clinic with other doctors, she probably can. Similarly, nothing prevents a lawyer from opening a solo practice or starting a new firm. A CPA might work for a company but might also have his own office.

To be sure, American religious history is replete with individuals who have started their own churches. However, in order for religious groups to persist over time, some degree of institutionalization is necessary. The original animating impulse, Weber's "charisma," must be "routinized" in order to produce the kind of stability necessary for long-term survival. Both churches and writing centers can and should have a prophetic mission; they are places where renewal, innovation, and boundary breaking can challenge the existing order. But both are also places that require accommodation, compromise, and an ability to test the institutional waters.

A final similarity between the writing center and the church has to do with their status as consecrated space. Both the writing center and the church are places where people congregate for specific purposes. Church is not the only place where worship occurs, but church is a special place set aside for worship, for fellowship, for reflection, admonishment, instruction. While all those activities can and do take place elsewhere, there seems to be some value in designating or consecrating certain places that will nurture those activities and their appropriate habits of mind. Similarly, while people can and do write or talk about writing in many places, there seems to be some value in creating special places set aside for those activities and their appropriate habits of mind. Just as both ministers and tutors experience a tension between being set apart or fellow pilgrims, so too do churches and writing centers occupy a space that is both set apart and common, both sacred and profane.

Like most churches, writing centers declare themselves open to any and all. And like most churches, particular writing centers develop an outreach to their own communities that reflects a complex blend of ideologies, personalities, and institutional and demographic realities. The result is pluralism. Just as American religious pluralism is a sign of a healthy democracy, so too should the variety among writing centers be seen as a sign of health. Let us celebrate our differences and affirm our commonalties as we seek to energize those metaphorically complex places we call writing centers.

Notes

[1] Because there is such a male-dominated cast to most of my citations regarding the clergy, I have retained language that I personally find sexist. Female clergy, though their ranks are increasing in some Protestant denominations, are still a small minority. Although Ann Douglas has argued convincingly that the professional ministry underwent a process of "feminization" that began in the nineteenth century, that process has not yet led to a significant female presence among employed clergy. This is one obvious area where the church is different from the writing center, where directors are 74% female (Healy).

Works Cited

Beecher, Henry Ward. "Sphere of the Christian Minister." *The Church and the City: 1865-1910.* Ed. Robert D. Cross. Indianapolis: Bobbs-Merrill, 1967. 154-81.

Bruffee, Kenneth A. "Peer Tutoring and the 'Conversation of Mankind.'" *Writing Theory and Administration.* Ed. Gary A. Olson. Urbana: NCTE, 1984. 3-15.

Carino, Peter. "Early Writing Centers: Toward a History." *The Writing Center Journal* 15.2 (1995): 103-15.

—. "What Do We Talk About When We Talk About Our Metaphors: A Cultural Critique of Clinic, Lab, and Center." *The Writing Center Journal* 13.1 (1992): 31-42.

Cox, Harvey. *The Secular City: Secularization and Urbanization in Theological Perspective.* New York: Macmillan, 1965.

Dittes, James. *The Church in the Way.* New York: Scribner's, 1967.

Douglas, Ann. *The Feminization of American Culture.* New York: Avon, 1977.

Ellingsen, Mark. "Luther's Concept of the Ministry: The Creative Tension." *Word & World* 1 (1981): 338-46.

Galbraith, John Kenneth. *The New Industrial State.* New York: Signet, 1967.

Gannon, Thomas M. "Priest/Minister: Profession or Non-Profession?" *Review of Religious Research* 12 (1971): 66-79.

Healy, Dave. "Writing Center Directors: An Emerging Portrait of the Profession." *WPA: Writing Program Administration* 18.3 (1995): 26-43.

Hemmeter, Thomas. "The 'Smack of Difference': The Language of Writing Center Discourse." *The Writing Center Journal* 11.1 (1990): 35-48.

Hobson, Eric H. "Writing Center Practice Often Counters Its Theory. So What?" *Intersections.* Ed. Joan A. Mullin and Ray Wallace. Urbana: NCTE, 1994. 1-10.

Kraemer, Hendrik. *A Theology of the Laity.* London: Lutterworth, 1958.

Lakoff, George, and Mark Johnson. *Metaphors We Live By.* Chicago: U of Chicago P, 1980.

Lazerwitz, Bernard. "A Comparison of Major United States Religious Groups." *The Social Meanings of Religion*. Ed. William M. Newman. Chicago: Rand McNally, 1974. 127-43.

Leahy, Richard. "Of Writing Centers, Centeredness, and Centrism." *The Writing Center Journal* 13.1 (1992): 43-52.

Logan, James C. "Ministry as Vocation and Profession." *Quarterly Review* 2 (1982): 5-26.

Lunsford, Andrea. "Collaboration, Control, and the Idea of a Writing Center." *The Writing Center Journal* 12.1 (1991): 3-10.

Niebuhr, H. Richard. *The Social Sources of Denominationalism*. New York: Holt, 1929. New York: Meridian, 1957.

North, Stephen. "The Idea of a Writing Center." *College English* 46.5 (1984): 433-46.

—. "Letters." *The Writing Center Journal* 15.2 (1995): 183-85.

—. "Revisiting 'The Idea of a Writing Center.'" *The Writing Center Journal* 15.1 (1994): 7-19.

Pemberton, Michael A. "The Prison, the Hospital, and the Madhouse: Redefining Metaphors for the Writing Center." *Writing Lab Newsletter* 17.1 (Sept. 1992): 11-16.

Riley, Terrance. "The Unpromising Future of Writing Centers." *The Writing Center Journal* 15.1 (1995): 20-34.

Sauls, Albert L. "The Ministry: Background, Present Trends." *Brethren Life and Thought* 20 (1975): 83-88.

Trimbur, John. "Peer Tutoring: A Contradiction in Terms?" *The Writing Center Journal* 7.2 (1987): 21-28.

Troeltsch, Ernst. *The Social Teaching of the Christian Churches*. Trans. Olive Wyon. New York: Macmillan, 1931.

Updike, John. *A Month of Sundays*. Greenwich: Fawcett Crest, 1975.

Weber, Max. *The Protestant Ethic and the Spirit of Capitalism*. Trans. Talcott Parsons. New York: Scribner's, 1958.

Winter, Gibson. *The Suburban Captivity of the Churches*. New York: Macmillan, 1962.

Winter, J. Alan. *Continuities in the Sociology of Religion: Creed, Congregation, and Community*. New York: Harper & Row, 1977.

Walking the Tightrope: Negotiating Between the Ideal and the Practical in the Writing Center

Albert C. DeCiccio
Michael J. Rossi
Kathleen Shine Cain

Merrimack College

To paraphrase literary critic Terry Eagleton, without some form of theory, however unreflective and implicit, people in higher education would not know what a writing center is (viii). Those of us who work in writing centers have debated what seems frequently to be every possible variation of tutoring and collaborative learning in our discussions of theory and descriptions of practice. In debating our differences, we have also grown more aware of our sense of common cause, come increasingly to recognize the controlling influence of institutional context, and begun to accept the diversity of our perspectives as a rich and constructive resource for development. It would not be unreasonable to suggest that the dynamic interplay between the ideal and the real that gives writing center theory its vitality depends on the willingness of individual centers to, in the words of a popular song, "Stand in the place where you are." It is by situating the idea of a writing center where it is put to work that the most appropriate theory emerges. In other words, while writing center theorists debate with one another, a parallel conversation among tutors and tutees is constructing real theory.

Consider briefly the visions that have been fashioned and espoused as the idea of a writing center. This representation is by no means all-inclusive, but several points can be made with it. The first is that the visions are estimable; we believe in them and aspire to affirm them. They point out the direction writing centers want to follow. The writing center is not the next best thing in writing instruction; it is the best next thing in, well, education. The second point is that ideas have a way of becoming stripped of complexity, rigidified, and rendered monolithic as they become popularized. As a result, they can become disabling rather than enabling, inducements to deny rather than to deal with unconforming realities. Moreover, we may end up alienating those with whom we work (writers) and for whom we work (colleges and universities, including all faculties, especially those who teach "writing"). The third and final point is that there are differences among us that the visions present. These differences may be disconcerting to those places desirous of either erecting or altering their own writing centers; alternately, they may form the basis upon which, through the kind of practice that informs new theory, writing centers grow.

Not long ago, Valerie Balester drew the line for writing center workers. In fact, she declared war on the *founding fathers* of the "CCCC Statement on Principles and Standards," saying that the Statement presents "an image of writing centers as supplemental to the English department curriculum, useful for training graduate teaching assistants and lightening the burden on faculty by giving their students individual attention. In other words, for service" (167). Later in the same piece, Balester wrote about "a self-proclaimed 'departmental compositionist' who goes under the pseudonym Hugh Campbell. He has," she said," ... given us a vision worthy of writing centers, placing them at the 'hub' of a university writing program, 'a place where writers of all levels ... can come for help, feedback, conversation about the art and craft of writing'" (170). This is, of course, the ideal center, the place writing center workers long to inhabit, the place where "writing is not only critiqued but also discussed, produced, researched, and enjoyed" (170).

Balester's statement is a wonderful way to set up a writing center as different than it's too often perceived: A writing center is not a fix-it shop. Balester offers a wonderful vision for what the writing center is ideally. Yet, do theorists who talk like Balester risk alienating colleagues in the English Department when they imply that we can teach them how to teach writing? In struggling to reach the ideal Balester describes, we send mixed messages to students who hear one thing in the writing classroom and another in the writing center. For example, if writing centers don't provide service, as Balester implies, what happens to those writers who require, or who have been required to seek, service?

Even the most recent of writing center theorists look to Ken Bruffee when they offer new visions of the writing center. They do so because Bruffee has exclaimed repeatedly that collaborative learning, peer tutoring, writing center work can inspire positive change. In *A Short Course on Writing*, for example, he writes,

> ... I aspire ... to contribute to an effort to redefine the roles of student and teacher, and to restructure the human relationship between people who want to learn and those whose calling it is to help them learn. The goal of that redefinition is still to help students gain authority over their knowledge and gain independence in using it. Its basic assumption is that a necessary

intermediate step on the way to effective independence is effective interdependence. (v)

Here, and elsewhere, Bruffee provides new hope for students stuck in the traditional paradigm that produced many of their teachers. However, the question arises: Should a writing center be authorized to change the pedagogy of the academy?

True, Bruffee should be credited for offering his ideas about the social nature of language and writing, fitting in his collaborative learning pedagogy as a result. According to Bruffee,

> Collaborative learning is a way of developing and focusing a resource that many of the more familiar approaches to teaching composition overlook: peer influence. In tapping this resource, collaborative learning makes some assumptions about the nature of reading and writing that differ from the assumptions made by most familiar ways of teaching composition. Composition textbooks tend to proceed on the assumption that reading and writing are solitary, individual acts. [I assume] that reading and writing are social, collaborative acts. [My aim] is to help students learn to write better by becoming members of an active, constructive community of writers and readers. (1)

What exactly does Bruffee mean by an active, constructive community of writers and readers? Could he mean the academy's definition of the same? In fact, some theorists have recently questioned Bruffee, seeing his pedagogy as a way to acculturate writers to mainstream written English. If this is an accurate criticism, then we may want to reconsider what it is we are "changing" writers to do.

Another early writing center theorist, Stephen North, told the academic world that the role of the tutor is

> to interfere, to get in the way, to participate in ways that will leave the ritual forever altered .... Occasionally we manage to convert ... writers from people who have to see us to people who want to .... It would be nice if in writing, as in so many things, people would do what we tell them because it's good for them, but they don't .... On the other hand, we do ... far too much work with writers whose writing has received caustic, hostile, or otherwise unconstructive commentary. (433-46)

Writing centers owe North a lot. After all, he gave us a *raison d'être*. Yet, he also presumes to give us who work in the center a singular authority over writers. But what is it that writing centers are authorizing and what (and who) may be excluded as a result?

Recently, Andrea Lunsford has provided a critique of Bruffee, cautioning people to see the danger that collaboration may lead to homogeneity; wanting dissensus not consensus necessarily, Lunsford writes,

> ... I think we must be cautious in rushing to embrace collaboration, because collaboration can also be used to reproduce the status quo; the rigid hierarchy of teacher-centered classrooms is replicated in the tutor-centered writing center in which the tutor is still the seat of all authority but is simply pretending it isn't so. Such a pretense of democracy sends badly mixed messages. It can also lead to the kind of homogeneity that squelches diversity, that waters down ideas to the lowest common denominator, that erases rather than values difference. This tendency is particularly troubling given our growing awareness for the roles gender and ethnicity play in all learning. So regression toward the mean is not a goal I seek in an idea of a writing center based on collaboration. (4)

Lunsford's is a useful critique, fashioned after years of writing center practice Lunsford has experienced. Yet, how many of us really think that the writing center model she criticizes is regressive?

Again, like those cited above, Lunsford's ultimate vision, her idea of a writing center, is wonderful. She announces,

> The idea of a center informed by a theory of knowledge as socially constructed, of power and control as constantly negotiated and shared, and as collaboration as its first principle presents quite a challenge. It challenges our way of organizing our center, of training our staff and tutors, and of working with teachers. It even challenges our sense of where we "fit" into this idea. More importantly, however, such a center presents a challenge to higher education, an institution that insists on rigidly controlled individual performance, on evaluation as punishment, on isolation. (5)

Yet is it in our best interest to seek her ideal by challenging? Making a move is admirable and even courageous, but writing center theorists like Lunsford should be certain that everyone in the writing center fully supports that move.

Nancy Grimm has gone beyond North, providing another idea of a writing center, one that had been planted by both Bruffee and North. And her idea is, like Lunsford's, fashioned on years of practice in the center:

> One of North's central arguments is that the essence of writing center method is talk, a point few would contest. Yet he also maintains that "a writing center is an institutional response" to the need of writers to talk about their writing. In the margin next to that statement, I wrote "since when do institutions respond to such needs?" The talk that occurs in writing centers is often the kind of talk that is difficult to sustain in institutional space–it is playful, non-instrumental, multidimensional and multi-vocal. It is the kind of talk that I struggle and often fail to develop in my classroom space. Yet educational institutions generally promote functional talk, and they fund writing centers because they want to develop functional literacy. The unhappy metaphors of hospital, clinic, and prison that haunt writing centers are a result of the notion that writing centers are institutional mechanisms .... One of North's key arguments is that writing centers do not exist "to serve, supplement, back up, complement, reinforce, or otherwise be defined by any external curriculum." Yet writing center work *is* defined by the curriculum in unavoidable ways because students come to us for help interpreting the curriculum. (5)

Perhaps we need to ask ourselves what exactly is wrong with teaching functional writing. Further, we should consider what will be erected in place of the curriculum. Later, in addressing what writing centers must do, Grimm suggests that we erect more theory:

> Writing center research has avoided ... issues because of unexamined promises and philosophies. The goal of our research should be to open a dialogue with English departments and with the institution as a whole, to rethink the way we practice literacy, to renegotiate a relationship with teachers of writing. It should help us think about how we might *change* the context of teaching because of what we learn about students .... When North's essay was published eight years ago, it provided a much needed self-validation for people who worked in writing centers. It is time, however, to stop talking only to ourselves. (6).

It is true that we need to do more than talk to ourselves. Grimm is levying an important charge; however, if research is the way we change, how valid is her suggestion that, in erecting new theory, writing center scholars won't be talking only to writing center scholars?

The visions of the writing center espoused by Balester, Bruffee, North, Lunsford, Grimm, and most current writing center professionals have in common a distancing of the ideal writing center from the remedial centers of the past. Such distancing of new ideal/new practice from old ideal/old practice is a standard part of establishing new movements and new theory in the academy. For writing centers, it has meant the opportunity to define their identity as communities of and for writers rather than fix-it shops, and it has created the space in which to strive to achieve our visions of the ideal writing center. As institutions have come around to accepting writing centers as more than fix-it shops, however, we are vexed to find writing centers pressed still to service functional literacy.

Students still come seeking help with grammar, punctuation, and spelling; faculty and administration still look to the writing center to fill the instructional void that surrounds functional literacy in the academy. These demands are easily rebuffed, perhaps too easily, by explaining that remediation is not really what writing centers are about. More problematic is the center that suspends theory to pull from its files tired workbook exercises to pacify demand. Such responses ultimately serve neither students nor writing centers well. The genuine underlying need remains unmet or no better than poorly met at some cost to the integrity of the center.

We are, moreover, especially chagrined when pressed to service functional literacy from quarters where our vision of the writing center has seemingly gained acceptance: by students whose growth as writers has kindled in them a new awareness of and genuine desire for greater mastery of standard English, by faculty who have seen the value to their students of the writing center as a community of writers but who also believe essential a level of functional literacy, by deans who recognize and value the center's contribution to the institution's intellectual atmosphere and academic life while their concerns about retention lead them to ask what the center is doing to help retain less functionally literate students, and so on. Citing the theoretical dichotomy between ideal and remedial writing centers in such cases will not suffice, for the response reveals itself as nakedly inadequate.

Perhaps we should instead interpret the increasing acceptance of writing centers as more than fix-it shops as both a mark of success in defining the modern writing center theoretically as other than remedial and also as a challenge to find ways consistent with our vision of the writing center to meet the legitimate needs of students for help in developing functional literacy. Current theory does not provide an answer—at least not an easily and widely accepted answer—to this challenge by posing an either-or choice: either community of writers or remedial center, progressive or reactionary. It is time to move past dichotomies in theorizing writing centers, time to explore what it might mean to be *more* than a remedial center instead of just *other* than.

What are the legitimate needs of students for practical assistance in developing functional literacy–for information, support, encouragement, and learning opportunities? How can writing centers meet those needs in a manner consistent with our ideals? In her call for more research and stronger emphasis on theory, Nancy Grimm admonishes us to avoid talking only to ourselves, to broaden the conversation to include English departments and other faculty and administrators. We are not likely, however, to find answers to these questions in dialogue with English departments, valuable as such dialogue would surely prove. English departments unfortunately have yet to face similar questions regarding their own responsibilities in relation to functional literacy. Nor are we likely to find answers in talking to ourselves, at least to ourselves as theorists or as writing center professionals. But we may begin to find answers and the basis for more theory in informed practice, especially by talking and listening to those caught in the middle between theory and daily demands to service functional literacy: our tutors. Sadly, Grimm's theoretical broader conversation, as played out at NCTE, CCCC, and the recent NWCA conference, too often ignores these key players in writing center operation.

Virtually all writing centers rely on non-faculty tutors, and most employ peer tutors. How are we to construct a writing center that accommodates the needs of the institution while maintaining philosophical integrity without considering the contribution of those who do most of the work of writing centers? The metaphor may be unfortunate, but tutors are the soldiers on the front lines, in the trenches, while writing center directors and faculty are the generals–sometimes they engage in the battle, but for the most part they take care of planning. One need only recall Pickett's charge to realize that leaving all decision-making to those the most removed from the fray can be devastating not only to the campaign but to those engaged in it as well.

How are those tutors who are responsive to the genuine service needs of students and who are committed to the ideal writing center, as defined by theory and by their directors, negotiating the conflicting demands confronting them in the writing center? What are their successes, misgivings, frustrations, and insights? Where can the benefit of their experience lead us as we reflect on theory with them, with ourselves, with English departments, and with our institutions?

At Merrimack College the conversation about negotiating between our theory and the reality of our institutional constructs has taken place among tutors for years. In the tutors' log, an on-line interactive journal, tutors engage in discussion designed to work through the thorny issues we address in scholarly journals and conferences. During the fall of 1990, the conversation was particularly fruitful. As we attempt to determine the relative merits of adhering to theory as opposed to conceding our service role, we might do well to listen to those who walk that tightrope daily.

In October of 1990, DMJ complains on the log that students want "proofreading services," and that when apprised of "the true nature of the Writing Center as a process and writing oriented structure, most refuse to stay.," In response, jvp offers this advice:

> ... usually a student who comes in asking help with grammar really needs help in other areas .... I usually approach this situation by telling them our philosophy and then saying well I can look over your paper and try to help you out. This way I don't refuse to work with anyone and they do not feel like I'm unwilling to work with them 'cause they have the "grammar disease." What usually happens is that we wind up having a dialogue about the ideas, content, organization; everything but grammar. Then when we have discussed all this they bring up grammar .... By using different approaches you can get around the "grammar disease" and help them with the paper.

Granted, jvp is approaching the problem from the standpoint of the practitioner, but she is certainly, to use a popular term, a *reflective* practitioner. Other tutors, however, are more comfortable with the theory. Consider CLV's response to the question of how to deal with the "grammar disease":

> Remember, the idea of collaborative writing is still a basically new and radical philosophy. I mean, look at academe: it's an institution that has been standing for years, untouched. I think it will take some time for the idea to really get through to everyone .... I think it's important to remember that we're here to introduce a process: a process of writing and critiquing, where peers influence peers and ideas are generated .... I think suggestion is the key word .... If you get the person involved, they have a personal stake in it. They react–it's really amazing, don't ya think? And, if they are used to being told the "right" answer, and they are used to proofreading, freak 'em out. Say something like

"Okay, what do you think about the paper? Are you comfortable with it?" .... There are a few subversive-type ways around grammar, etc. People are comfortable with being told what to do. But, if you give them a chance to react, to talk about themselves, their ideas, they really begin to enjoy it. Once they get over the fear of 1) being judged, 2) getting "corrected," 3) getting it right; they do pretty well .... **It's a process, not a rule!!!** Grammar is a part of the writing process—face it! However, it's one of the very last steps to the process. Once you gain confidence about the process and the concepts, the grammar sort of takes care of itself–at least if you do a few drafts it does .... INTERNALIZATION—I realize we're all very afraid of "buzzwords," but I really do believe in the process .... Don't be afraid of the philosophy: you can get around people who want to work on grammar—get them involved in their ideas!!!

"It's a process, not a rule!!!" It's interesting that CLV, a college junior at the time, recognizes what some of us on the professional side have only just come to appreciate: that in part because of their academic nature, writing centers run the risk of becoming as monolithic in their pedagogy as the traditional academy. And her admonition against fear of philosophy speaks volumes about the daily trials of tutors who are taught, on the one hand, that the center's philosophy is inviolate, and who experience, on the other, students and faculty who treat them as service workers. Her ability to negotiate the dangerous ground between those two positions is worthy of our attention; she may well have something to teach those of us seeking that elusive connection between theory and practice.

Another approach to the theory/reality question is offered by RDH, a professional tutor with a degree in humanities. RDH refers to the advice a poet gave his students: "You'll never be a poet until you realize that everything I say today and this quarter is wrong. It may be right for me, but it is wrong for you .... your most important arguments are with yourself." Exploring this idea, RDH offers another observation that many of us forget as we converse among ourselves and with other faculty: "One thing about grammar and spelling ... is that they are the only words that many people know about writing. Ask someone how his process is. He won't know what you're talking about." As RDH remind us, as we determine how we negotiate our position with regard to the needs of the academy, we must recall North's admonition that writing centers exist for writers, not for institutions. In theory, of course, the institution exists for students as well. Perhaps, then, we might heed the advice of our students and peer tutors as we argue over the appropriate philosophy.

If we believe in collaborative theory enough to insist that our tutors use it with student writers, then why don't we use it in our discussions of writing center theory? Why aren't our tutors more involved in the conversation? Their observations on the subject, developed from their reflections on actual tutorials, can be enlightening. Consider, for example, CLV's observation at the end of the semester-long log discussion:

> Whether we like it or not, we are agents of institutional change–we are helping people to learn. We get students involved in a process by which they can enhance their writing and internalize it so that they can apply it elsewhere. Okay, it's fine to say that you disagree with a certain position someone takes about theory, but I personally would like to see more people write [in the log] about more ACTUAL tutorial sessions .... It's okay to debate theory, as long as you don't lose sight of where the philosophy is really working: it works in sessions in the Center, in the programs outside the Center, and hopefully in the minds of the students we guide. No one really holds the book on tutoring. But, through a dialogue with each other–digress, a dialogue which benefits everyone and not just the people arguing, we can learn more about this philosophy and how it works IN AND OUT OF THE CENTER ...

A less passionate example can be found in comments offered by cg, who until now has remained silent on the question. Lest the ranks be divided between those who espouse theory and those who focus on practice, cg offers his assessment of the purpose of the conversation:

> But what's going on in here is a direct result of the theory we are attempting to put into practice, a theory you yourself call radical. And if there's a "practical" problem in here—especially if it's a recurring problem—we can probably remedy it by rethinking and reexamining our philosophy. The grammar thing is a perfect example. The debate has continued for so long because a lot of us are concerned about it. I think this is exactly the kind of thing we should address in the log. And even if we can't reach a consensus, we can rethink our own opinion on the matter–and put it into practice in our tutorials. I think your implication that we are debating for the sake of debate is a bit severe .... The log, as I see it, is a type of forum where tutors can share their ideas and experiences on tutoring. Isn't that right? And isn't that exactly what we're doing?

The log for Fall 1990 provided the impetus for tutors to embark upon a revision of the tutor training handbook. Highlighting the introductory material in the new handbook is a section titled "Theory," which spells out the consensus arrived at during the course of the conversation on theory versus reality:

> Tutors will encounter writers with many different needs. It is the responsibility of each tutor to be responsive to these needs. This can be done in various ways. Since many instructors use methods and philosophies different than those of the Writing Center, tutors need to attempt, through collaboration, to find out how they can best benefit the writer in a session. Attempting to overtly convert the writer or the professor to the collaborative view is not always productive and can impede open conversation. Instead, the tutor should discover, through dialogue with the writer, which method will best help him or her. The following paragraphs are examples of various models for tutoring sessions. Most sessions are not pure examples of any one particular philosophy, but rather use elements from many different models in order to find a combination that best fits individual student writing processes.

The tutors' assertion that "many instructors use methods and philosophies different than those of the Writing Center" is tempered by their acknowledgment that "attempting to convert ... is not always productive and can impede open conversation." What tutors have learned, it seems, from their tightrope walk is that it may well be possible to negotiate between the ideal and the real—so long as we keep in clear focus the primary purpose of the center.

The kind of debate that DMJ, jvp, RDH, CLV, cg, and others engaged in during Fall 1990 may use the language of the uninitiated, but it's hard to overlook the sophistication of their arguments. Their articulation of writing center theory and practice in the revised handbook illustrates precisely what all of us try to do as we seek to marry theory to practice. Because they spend their days walking the tightrope between the ideal and the practical, they have become adept at accommodation, subversion, and negotiation. The conversation begun by Bruffee and North and continued by Lunsford and Grimm is paralleled, we believe, by the conversation going on every day among tutors in writing centers across the country. The one thing we all seem able to agree upon is the legitimacy of collaborative theory. It's high time, then, that we put our money where our mouth (or pen) is, and truly listen to those who live the theory we preach.

Works Cited

Balester, Valerie. "Revising the Statement: On the Work of Writing Centers." *College Composition and Communication* 44 (1992): 167-71.

Bruffee, Kenneth A. *A Short Course in Writing.* 3rd ed. Boston: Little, Brown, 1985.

Eagleton, Terry. *Literary Theory: An Introduction.* Minneapolis: U of Minnesota P, 1983.

Grimm, Nancy. "Contesting 'The Idea of a Writing Center': The Politics of Writing Center Research." *Writing Lab Newsletter* 17.1 (1992): 5-7.

Lunsford, Andrea. "Collaboration, Control, and the Idea of a Writing Center." *Writing Lab Newsletter* 16.4-5 (1991/92): 1-5.

North, Stephen M. "The Idea of a Writing Center." *College English* 46 (1984): 433-46.

Writing Centers
and Writing Assessment:
A Discipline-Based Approach

Mark L. Waldo
Jacob Blumner
Mary Webb

University of Nevada

In a 1990 *College Composition and Communications* article about writing assessment, Ed White addresses an issue of importance to anyone engaged in writing across the curriculum or assessment. "We are caught," he observes, "in the languages we speak and in the discourse communities of our disciplines." For White, being "caught" in these communities is a problem because they isolate us one from the other: "…the language specializations that largely define our disciplines and allow us to work as 'professionals' also cut us off from other important communities." On the one hand, language specializations define the disciplines and allow us to work as professionals, each a necessary characteristic of writing and research in a university department; on the other hand, these specializations "cut us off" from each other with the consequence that "we do not see or read or value these other communities …. " (191). White's awareness of difference in academic communities is broad enough for him to poke confessional fun at himself: "… I often work professionally with those in other disciplines, but I confess that my PhD in English literature has so confirmed a particular discourse community that I routinely (and this is the point: notice how routinely it happens, even in this paper) find it hard to respect the scholarship of non-literary communities" (191). White is alert to his own confirmation in a literary community and its potential impact on his work with others; this awareness probably helps him to treat other communities with fairness.

Not seeing, not reading, not valuing the languages that define other communities, however, has obvious implications for WAC. Rhetorical conventions, language and thinking patterns themselves, are largely defined by the discipline in which, to borrow Thomas Kuhn's term, academics and professionals have "gone native" (204). WAC personnel are almost always from one discipline, and they will carry the burden of viewing the academic world through that discipline's language, its frames for thinking and writing. They need to be aware of how that view shapes their thinking in order to work fairly and not prescriptively (or colonially) with those immersed in other language environments. White's comments also have significant implications for assessment of student writing competence. They suggest the potential difficulties in the "one test/ measurement instrument fits all" approach to writing assessment. If separate language specializations define our disciplines and allow us to work as professionals, how can members from one discipline capably and fairly define the competence of student writers in another? White's essay prepares us for this large and, given how much global assessment is done by local departments, ominous question, but it delivers on a much smaller issue.

In the 1990 article, White seems far more concerned with the language differences experts in assessment might have than differences between academic communities or problems with one test fitting all. "The choice of an evaluator," he argues compellingly, "often means the selection of a unique set of assumptions and definitions that emerge out of the language of the evaluator's world; the implications of such a choice … can be profound, affecting funding or even the survival of the program." With the choice of an evaluator, schools also select a unique, language-based set of assumptions emerging from the evaluator's world. What impact will the evaluator's assumptions have on the scoring of the essays? Will the evaluator's confirmation in one language, in a slight revision of White's confession about himself, cause him or her to lack respect for the writing of students from another community? White prepares us for these questions, exposing a serious potential problem with assessment: Who is to do it? From what set of assumptions? How can those assumptions cross disciplines? He then aims, however, at a narrower target—linguistic/conceptual differences between the measurement community in education and the writing community in English.

There is no doubt he's right as far as the micro-picture goes. The College of Education's "value-added" and "value free" assessment, particularly if it is (as he remarks) "amateurish, filled with another discipline's jargon, expressing ambiguities and untested assumptions" (197), is going to be dismissed as "inappropriate measurement; not data, but data misused" (198) by a community versed in composition studies. Professionals in composition will certainly value some features of student writing more, some less than testers in education. On the macro-point, however, the point that asks how the electrical engineering student can be measured as a writer by education or English, White misses the mark or ignores it.

And that problem is the one we are trying to solve through the writing center at the University of Nevada: how to avoid blanket assessment, the testing and grading of students in all majors from one department's perspective. Our WAC program (Waldo 15-27) is essentially discipline based, meaning that the goals, purposes, and forms for writing are discovered in the disciplines themselves, not translated or imposed from one discipline to another. With White, we accept that each discipline, in greater or lesser degrees of distinction, has its own frames for thinking, speaking, and writing. Each department is its own language community. Perhaps in a slight qualification of White's position we believe that no one community's frames are better than any other's.

Our WAC program, in practice, draws out what *faculty* value about writing and the goals *they* have for using writing in class, helping them to translate their values and goals into assignments and grading techniques. This approach has experienced wide acceptance and dramatic growth during the last five years. Where before 1989 very little writing was included in classes outside the humanities, writing center statistics indicate that every department now uses writing assignments in some of its courses, some departments use writing in every course, and minimally 700 classes have substantial writing components as part of their pedagogy. We attribute these results to the main advantage of the discipline-based program: it invests faculty in the meaningful use of writing because it makes them responsible for every aspect of its use. Students also invest in the writing of their discipline, its values, its purposes, its forms, and not some bowdlerized version of that writing. With Charles Bazerman, we think that writing in the context of the discipline is helping move, say, the neophyte chemistry major into the cognitive and language frames of the practicing chemist.

Things have progressed well in terms of setting up the WAC program and making it a part of our institution's fabric. In the spring of 1993, after four years of writing center presence and WAC activity, many of us (administrators, teachers, writing center personnel) became interested in assessing the quality of writing students were doing and the quality of assignment making. Because of the nature of our program, the question was how to assess. Many universities, particularly to the west of us, use timed writing tests or upper-division writing classes to measure writing competence. Perhaps one of these two approaches would suit us.

We examined the Graduation Writing Assessment Requirement (GWAR) used by the California State University System because it seemed typical of assessment across the US, combining timed writing tests with writing classes in English or the disciplines. According to a document (1988) explaining GWAR, the assessment requirement was satisfied at two California State University campuses by completion of a designated course; five campuses required the completion of an examination at an acceptable level; eight campuses required the completion of an examination or a course; and four campuses required the completion of an examination and a course.

Typically, the timed exam under the GWAR umbrella lasts sixty minutes to three hours, essays written from one or two questions or prompts. It often includes an objective portion: subjects, verbs, objects, fragments, comma splices, semi-colons, word choices. One of the essay exams is described this way: "Within the one hour time frame, students are required to plan their work for five minutes, write for 40, and review and edit for 15." These exams are largely administered and graded by English faculty.

We discovered many problems with them. For instance, how can any binding claims be made about writing ability based on five minutes for planning, forty minutes for writing, and fifteen minutes for editing? The psychometricists who maintain that no one test is reliable enough to make lasting decisions about students must certainly object to this format. And yet global decisions are often made about students based on this very local test. Further, haven't we known conclusively for more than thirty years that objective treatment of the features of standard written English has no effect for improving the quality of writing students do? So, if we're measuring writing ability, why the objective portion of the test?

This approach to assessment was easy to dismiss for us, not only because global decisions about students cannot ethically (or psychometrically) be made but also because of Ed White's caution: Who writes these tests and who evaluates them? From what set of assumptions, values, cultural contexts are they drawn and graded? However hard test designers and graders try not to, they must see at least partially through the blinders of their discipline. This reality makes it virtually impossible to design or grade a "one size fits all test." Such a test is not only inconsistent with but antithetical to our program.

Taking a writing class seemed a far better approach to assessment than the timed test, for our program at least. Of the nineteen campuses in the CSU system, six appear to have GWAR writing courses within various disciplines. Seven offer upper-division writing courses through English exclusively or through one or two other departments: journalism, communications, foreign languages, history.

Taking classes approximates real writing situations more closely than timed exams. Students have time to write and revise, to collaborate with others, in a context that matters to them. Certainly, the writing done during a quarter or semester may be said to present better "evidence of writing ability" than the writing done during 60, 90, or 120 minutes. Even so, the class model for assessment would not suit our program either, for reasons less obvious than the timed tests. Our program recognizes that each discipline has its own relationship to language, comprises its own writing community. Upper division writing courses taught in humanities disciplines (English, communications, foreign languages, history) will present and evaluate writing from their community's point of view. This means that students who take these courses from other disciplines may be disadvantaged by membership in their discipline's language community, with its differing if not opposing frames for thinking and writing.

The problem would appear to be resolved by basing these writing courses in the disciplines themselves; thus students in biology take a writing class in biology, pass with a C- or better, and satisfy the graduation requirement (California State University, Chico). This situation is vastly preferable to the timed exam. It is also preferable to a class offered by one, two, or three departments. But it still will not be suitable to assess the writing of our students. Its unsuitability does not stem from any inherent wrong in it as a system for assessment but in its wrongness for our cross-curricular model. First, these writing courses are sometimes taught by adjuncts from other departments, as is our writing in engineering course (taught by English lecturers like Mary Webb); these instructors may well be first rate and try hard to teach their classes value free or oriented to values of the students in the course; but they can hardly help, as Ed White remarks, from seeing the world from their own rhetorical perspective. Second, when one or two classes are designated as writing classes within a department, the tendency in other classes is to give over responsibility for student writing to them. Our program endorses the use of writing in nearly every course, not a few writing intensive courses. We therefore had to reject these models in favor of a model designed to accommodate our WAC program.

We decided that we would invite the faculty from selected departments to assess the writing done by their junior and then senior students. These faculty members would form departmental assessment committees and would be paid a stipend of $750 for their participation. The two departments chosen for the pilot year (93-94) were criminal justice and electrical engineering. We selected criminal justice because it represents a growing number of departments nationwide in which small faculties deal with large numbers of students. Because of the obvious obstacles, writing is very often not assigned in classes offered by these departments. The criminal justice department at UNR has approximately 300 majors and only 5.5 faculty members to teach classes, and upper division classes often have over 100 students. Criminal Justice 326, "Juvenile Justice," averages over 85 students. Two CJ 320 classes, "Courts in Criminal Justice," have had 103 and 104 students in them, respectively, and the numbers continue to increase. Still, in the face of such discouraging figures, the faculty manages to incorporate writing into every class.

The CJ faculty members were interested in seeing how their students developed as writers, where they were weak as a group, and where they were strong. They also wanted to compare how they assessed their students' writing, which steps they could take to evaluate papers more consistently; how they could develop assignments to enhance critical thinking; and how they might alter their teaching to increase the amount of writing their students do.

After discussing these goals and what kind of paper collection was necessary, we decided to track 40 juniors through their criminal justice classes, and 10 of those through all of their classes, in order to provide the study with an adequate sample of upper-division student writing. In all cases, the portfolios of student papers would be numerically coded, the students anonymous. We spent the fall 1993 semester collecting the written work these students did including papers, exams and short essays. We designed collection to be as convenient as possible for instructors, contacting all instructors whose students were being tracked to confirm paper collection. Then, as due dates approached, we reminded the faculty of the collection and arranged for paper copying. In order to get papers before instructors marked and graded them, a student assistant met instructors at convenient times, copied the papers, and returned them immediately. The minimized inconvenience made faculty more willing to participate.

In our meetings, committee members evaluated the papers by assignment, shared rankings, and compared findings with other colleagues. Early criteria for assessment included the ability to develop a topic, to incorporate material from outside classes and sources, to organize a coherent essay, and to write with minimal sentence-level errors. Norming several sets of papers, we began to make some descriptive generalizations about student writing ability; the papers were judged largely successful in working with topics and organization, less successful in incorporating outside sources and writing error free. But it must be emphasized that these judgments were tentative, and that the process evolved as much toward assessment of faculty expectations and assignments as student writing. The committee decided that evidence of higher-order thinking skills (problem solving, examining opposing points of view, arguing convincingly) was the most commonly valued quality they sought.

They further determined that certain types of assignments were more likely to encourage these skills than others. The most successful assignment seen by the committee required students to incorporate three administrative qualities from Machiavelli's *The Prince* in order to argue for their promotion in a police force. The assignment had clear goals and a specific audience, and it provided an engaging context for writing about

The Prince—arguing for their own promotion. When asked, the professor noted that 90% of the papers fulfilled the requirements successfully, an extraordinary figure born out by the 10 papers (out of 100) the committee read and ranked.

The assignment that produced the least successful writing was very open ended, allowing students to write about any topic of interest to them chosen from the subject of juvenile justice. Abstract in goals, audience and context, this assignment resulted in students' struggling with topics too broad and complex to be handled in the average five pages; consequently, topic development, use of outside sources, and organization lacked accordingly. After six months of reading criminal justice papers with CJ faculty members, we have learned what common sense may have told us from the start: the types of writing assignments faculty make have much to do with the quality of the writing students do. The committee members believe their students, on the whole, are achieving the faculty's goals, and especially so when an assignment's goals are clear. By continuing this study, we hope to learn more about how well students are writing in criminal justice, and the relationship between assignment making and quality.

We had chosen electrical engineering for assessment for two reasons: their curriculum is a pre-professional one that focuses on the hard sciences—mathematics, physics, chemistry—as well as communication in the professional world; and we had informally been apprised of so much poor writing on the part of their students that we were interested to see what sort of writing they did. We planned to track 10 juniors through their remaining two years (again anonymously), collecting writing assignments from each of their instructors. We also decided to collect all of the papers written in five lab classes ranging from the 300 to 400 level, some of which, we learned later, included 10 to 12 lab reports per semester. The Assessment Committee would meet during the spring semester to read the papers we collected and develop criteria for successful writing in electrical engineering.

By the spring semester of 1994, we were ready to meet with the two faculty members from electrical engineering, one a tenured associate professor and the other an untenured assistant professor. We had managed to collect about 120 papers. The first batch of papers we looked at came from the untenured faculty member's course in digital systems (a 400-600 level course). The assignment was a final report, submitted by teams of students at the close of the semester when the device they had proposed to build had been completed. Thus, the assignment included the initial proposal for the design, a user's manual, a disclaimer, and parts list. The instructor who designed the assignment had shown the committee copies of his students' original proposals for their term projects—it was obvious that he had encouraged students to submit drafts for his response long before the final papers were due. He did an enormous amount of work with his students' writing, helping with both organizational and sentence-level problems. Six of the seven papers we looked at were "of publishable quality," according to committee members. There was a unanimous feeling that these students had received valuable feedback from the instructor and that this feedback had produced excellent papers.

The two electrical engineering committee members began, from the first meeting, to address characteristics valued in writing for their profession: writing must always be purposeful, clear, organized, and appropriate for its audience. They also paid attention to sentence level-errors and the difficulties of evaluating reports containing many second-language problems. Generally, as the meetings progressed, we spent time discussing issues that emerged from their own experience with publishing in professional journals. They expressed concern that their writing must precisely meet the dictates of target journals and shared "war stories" about how various editors responded to their work when it did not. Their feelings of anxiety about publishing perhaps translated into one of the unstated expectations they had for student writing: that it be perfect. Students rarely met this expectation, explaining some of the criticism being leveled at them as writers.

The most rewarding part of this project so far is our early conclusion that, where writing is included in the electrical engineering program, the results are very good; student writing is much better than the committee had expected. Faculty members remarked of many of the papers we normed that they "demonstrate the cleanest engineering while properly framing the problems"; they are "not only well-written, but contain creative ideas." Faculty members also described the writing with terms from their own rhetoric, saying of less successful papers that "the papers demonstrate a flat feature space," or that they lack what our rhetoric would term appropriate organization. So far we see, not surprisingly, that the farther into the EE program the student is, the better his or her writing.

When writing is used in EE classes, more often than anyone realized but probably still not often enough, it tends to be integrally linked to the teaching and learning. Students recognize that writing lab reports and team projects has value for their work at school and their jobs beyond. Understanding why they are writing and doing the large amounts of "hidden writing" that they do lead to surprisingly able writers and thinkers, at least when perfection is not the ultimate standard for assessment.

Our assessment project is experiencing losses and gains by comparison to the CSU GWAR project. The main loss is, of course, that we cannot assess every student. When you assess student writing by discipline, you cannot do them all without prohibitive expense. The advantage is that we prefer it that way, being able to concentrate on the writing of a limited number of students. Second, you lose control of the evaluative process, the faculty in the disciplines taking it from you. As we have questioned them about their values for writing, at first they were reluctant to respond, or to respond beyond the sentence level. During the course of our initial several weeks, however, they became more bold, describing in detail their expectations for students specifically and their language community generally. We were no longer allowed much latitude to speak, one member of the criminal justice committee actually telling one of us "not to talk so much." Third, our program, while portfolio based, insisted on the anonymity of student writers. We are collecting all the writing of 40 randomly selected junior CJ majors and 10 EE majors, along with all the writing included in each EE class that uses writing, but we cannot block any of the students from graduation. This, of course, we see as an advantage, too, given that our project is in its initial stages. We want faculty members within the disciplines to make any decisions regarding the graduation status of individual students, if such a decision is to be made. Fourth, we are limited to descriptive analyses of the writing students do. We have no control group from five years ago with which to compare experimental groups and assignments faculty make. This is an advantage that time testing can claim almost immediately, one year to the next. We regret that we cannot make comparative analyses before several years. But we also believe that this is the way that writing should be assessed, within the context of the discipline and over the course of several years.

Our most important conclusions for this initial report stem from its contrast to (what are now) standard procedures in assessment. We are fortunate to be able to evaluate student writing within the disciplines. As White so eloquently points out, universities are discipline-based language communities. Perhaps it is arguable whether they should be so. But it is inarguable, at least in the case of a university such as ours, that it is so. Since our WAC consultants work so hard to get faculty members to use writing within the context of their disciplines, we believe that, in fairness to the students, they must also assess its quality within that context.

Works Cited

Bazerman, Charles. "How Language Realizes the Work of Science." *Shaping Written Knowledge: The Genre and Activity of the Experimental Article in Science.* Madison: U of Wisconsin P, 1988.

Kuhn, Thomas. *The Structure of Scientific Revolutions.* Chicago: U of Chicago P, 1970.

Waldo, Mark L. "The Last Best Place for WAC: The Writing Center." *WPA: Writing Program Administrator* 16 (1993): 15-27.

White, Edward M. "Language and Reality in Writing Assessment." *College Composition and Communication* 41 (1990): 187-200.

Perceptions, Realities, and Possibilities: Central Administration and Writing Centers

Jeanne Simpson
Eastern Illinois University

Based on my interactions with writing center personnel over the past dozen years, and, I emphasize, not based on any empirical research, the following are among the most common perceptions that writing center personnel hold with regard to central administration:

1. Central Administration prefers to keep writing centers powerless and marginalized.

2. Central Administration is where all the power is concentrated.

3. Central Administration's distribution of funding support within an institution is unpredictable at best, capricious at worst.

4. Faculty rank and the situating of a writing center within a department accrue important prestige in the Central Administration.

5. Major curricular decisions are made in the Central Administration.

6. Retention, tenure, and promotion decisions are determined primarily by Central Administration.

Other perceptions also operate, but these are the most common and the ones upon which many writing center decisions about design, mission, staffing, and reporting tend to be made. It is important, therefore, to study these perceptions and to determine their accuracy.

To do that, perhaps the best place to go next is Central Administration and talk about its perceptions of writing centers.

1. Actual information, detailed and precise, that Central Administration has about writing centers tends to be fairly sparse, coming forward almost entirely by means of reports.

Administrators, by and large, are more burdened with paper pushing and meeting schedules than faculty imagine, so that opportunities to get out and visit campus facilities may be governed by crisis, not by desire to acquire knowledge.

The crisis may be a physical plant breakdown or a personnel difficulty, or it may be a more positive crisis, such as an accreditation site visit. But still a crisis—and thus a way of limiting and focusing what Central Administration will be looking at and therefore what they will see and not see.

Thick and detailed reports are not the solution to this problem. Rather, careful planning of what goes into the required reports and carefully timed invitations to Central Administration would be a more effective solution. The point is that writing centers have more control over what Central Administration knows about them than is perceived.

2. Central Administration is interested in information that addresses the issues that concern it.

These are things like accreditation, accountability (assessment), staffing plans, space allocation, and personnel dollars. Those are the nuts-and-bolts concerns, the daily assignment of administration. It is crucial to understand that.

Thus, a writing center for Central Administration is space, student use, personnel dollars, productivity, and a program that requires assessment and evaluation on the basis of institutional mission and priorities. Notice that the quality of instruction is in there, but not obviously and not at the head of the list. That does not mean that quality is not a concern of Central Administration. But the other issues are why Central Administration exists in the first place.

3. Assessment of instructional quality is the business of departments and the faculty of an institution. Central Administration is the place where "big picture" information about assessment is gathered, where the money and time and reporting lines for assessment are addressed. But not the assessment itself.

4. The concept of "marginalization" would be a surprise to Central Administration. If a program is being funded, space provided, salaries paid, assessment and evaluation being conducted, then the assumption of

Central Administration is that it is a part of the institution and that some part of the institution's mission is being addressed.

Now that doesn't mean that funds may not be distributed sparingly, that positions may be temporary. But what looks like marginalization from the writing center point of view will be regarded by Central Administration as keeping flexibility available for shifting funds, reallocating staffing positions, redistributing space. In times of budget shortages (and we can expect them for the foreseeable future), flexibility is not only wise, it is required.

"Marginal" then means what can be cut if a budget recisions occur. And they do occur. These decisions are often based on the available unspent or unencumbered funds. A prime target, for example, would be a summer school, if a recision came late in the fiscal year. On the other hand, support service cuts are risky, for they alienate students and reduce retention rates, which in turn will reduce income further. But Central Administration may need to be reminded of that.

The situation is not changed by this difference in perceptions. It is still unpleasant and limits options and possibilities. But the understanding of how to respond to the situation, the development of realistic and effective responses, depends on a clear understanding of how the check-signers perceive the situation. They do not perceive themselves as oppressors and tend to react defensively against such accusations. Even an intransigent, blockheaded Central Administration will react negatively to such accusations.

5. Central Administration considers most evaluation decisions (retention, promotion, tenure) to be primarily made at the department level.

The closest, most accurate, and most comprehensive sense of what is going on in a discipline, of what constitutes appropriate and effective scholarship and teaching methodology, and of what are meaningful professional activities, exists in departments and—in institutions that have them—divisions or colleges.

Central Administration will override recommendations made at lower levels, but infrequently. To be regularly at variance with these recommendations is to court dissension, protest, grievances, and lawsuits, none of which is considered desirable by Central Administration (though we face them daily).

Furthermore, it is in the best interests of good assessment and program review for these determinations to be made by knowledgeable people. Central Administration does have a vested interest in valid and positive assessment outcomes.

6. Departmental affiliation is not seen by Central Administration as a prestige issue but as a mechanical/organizational/logistical issue.

Because it is the most common structure, it is therefore the best understood. It determines how funding will be channeled, reporting lines established, and evaluation conducted. It is conventional, defined, and therefore not problematic: the line of least resistance. If a less conventional structure is to be pursued, these issues will have to be sorted out to the satisfaction of Central Administration, and clarity and efficiency should be among the criteria. A frequent difficulty for writing centers is that they do not easily fit the conventional structure and yet are jammed into it because it is familiar to both Central Administration and writing center staff.

An alternative response, also frequent, is to use temporary staffing and soft funding, as much out of inertia (what to do with this odd duck among the various programs?) as out of a desire for flexibility. When in doubt, stall, and these structures are the manifestations of stalling. Once you establish a tenure line and the related evaluation system, you have made a commitment not to move things around. Tenure-line positions mean that the institution is thinking about something for a very long haul. People are in a hurry to get tenure, and they are reluctant to leave once they have it. A tenure-line position is, when you consider it, an institutional commitment of at least 20 years' duration. That means, literally, thousands and thousands of dollars in salary and benefits. For Central Administration, whose responsibility is the prudent management of those dollars, it only makes sense to take a long, squinty-eyed look at any request for such commitment. It is generally not a desire to oppress or marginalize anybody.

Related to this responsibility is the one of supervising and adjusting the institutional structure so that all the parts fit together coherently and efficiently. Programs are not looked at in isolation, though the persons who are involved with them may have that perception. For Central Administration, a writing center may be a discrete unit, but not a separate one, one that fits into the whole. They must consider not just the content of the writing center's activities, but where it fits in the organizational structure. Where should it go? How will other units be affected? The flow of information? Decision-making authority? Funding? Equipment? Space?

Again, departmental affiliation is, superficially, the easiest answer to these questions. In some institutions, a deeper analysis may yield the same answer. But not always.

7. Finally, caprice is complicated and costly. It is very, very seldom what is behind a Central Administration decision. Rather, funding, in

whatever form, is at the bottom of *most* Central Administration decisions. Period. All decisions, including tenure, are ultimately budgetary in their implications. Caprice, on the other hand, leads to lawsuits and other difficulties. It creates unusual and time-consuming problems to be solved, distracting Central Administration from the routine work that must be done.

Of course I don't discount Murphy's Law and the Stupidity Factor from the decision-making process. But in analyzing why a Central Administration decision has been made, I urge the application of Occam's Law: the simplest explanation is the likeliest, and in this case, that means budget.

What then are the implications for writing centers and writing center personnel if we proceed from these observations?

The kind of information that writing center directors will need to gather and distribute will not be as closely related to the philosophy and daily functioning of a writing center as it will be to larger, institutional issues. Directors need to be sophisticated enough in their own administrative activities to balance the two levels of knowledge and expertise—theoretical and managerial, pedagogical and budgetary—effectively.

A problem that I see and that I hope will begin to be addressed by our professional literature and organizations is that the professional preparation of writing center personnel is very effective at covering the theoretical and the pedagogical and virtually silent on the managerial and budgetary. We want to strengthen our programs but have almost no good information or understanding of how to do so effectively.

Our idealism, one of the fuels that propels successful and innovative writing centers, is also a problem for us, leading us to misperceive our institutional situations and, frequently, to exacerbate problems by applying the wrong remedy. I would urge that careful study, a lot of talk and legwork, and, above all, the consistent requirement of looking at the whole institution, will be far and away the most effective way to end this matter of "marginalization" for writing centers. We need to adopt the principle that we use so often in tutoring: abandon our preconceived notions and look at what is actually there.

E Pluribus Unum: An Administrator Rounds Up Mavericks and Money

David E. Schwalm
Arizona State University West

This essay will demonstrate, through a site-specific account, the general values and concerns that a central administrator brings to the development of a writing center. Since sites provide different contexts and their administrators have different motives, the trick for the reader will be to separate the general from the particular, to determine what characteristics of this case study transcend the local circumstances and personalities. I'll try to help. In this case, the site is Arizona State University West, and I am the central administrator.

First, some essential background. Arizona State University West, located on the northwest side of Phoenix, is a separately accredited degree-granting campus of Arizona State University providing upper division and graduate education to about 5,000 students. ASU West has existed as a concept for 11 years, offered courses in malls, schools, and portables for seven years, and now operates from a beautiful urban campus completed in 1991. We received NCA accreditation in the fall of 1992. We have 22 bachelor's degree programs, an MBA, and several master's degrees in Education. Since the summer of 1992, I have served as Vice Provost for Academic Programs. As chief academic officer, my primary responsibility has been to guide the academic transition of ASU West from its former role as a branch campus offering bits and pieces of ASU Main programs to its new role as an autonomous, self-sufficient campus offering a full range of student services and complete degree programs.

This is a rare and wonderful opportunity—to be involved in building something new, to be dealing with the problems of growth rather than retrenchment, generally to be able to incorporate much of what we have learned about teaching and learning into the fundamental culture of the campus. There's a personal side as well. For 6 years, I served as writing program administrator at the Main campus—in a classic WPA situation: enormous amounts of responsibility and vulnerability and no authority or money. As Vice Provost, I still have enormous amounts of responsibility and vulnerability, but I also have some authority and money to go with it. It was nice to get up off my knees.

Anyway, after I lolled around my cushy office for a couple of days, ordered some business cards, and authorized myself to make a long distance call, I figured it was time to use my good fortune—while it lasted—to do at least one thing that would benefit the West campus for a long time. Rhetoric and composition have given me a delightful academic career and an interesting world view. Being a WPA prepared me better than any experience I can imagine to function effectively as a campus administrator. It was payback time—time to "do something" to support writing.

The students at ASU West made "doing something" to support writing highly desirable. The faculty, administration, and budget at ASU West made it possible.

Student Needs. Since ASU West is a non-residential upper division and graduate campus, all of our students commute, and all are transfer students—over 60% of them from five Maricopa Community College District campuses within a 20-mile radius, a big chunk from ASU Main (25 miles away), the rest from elsewhere. Our students are mostly first-generation college students, older on the average than undergraduates at more traditional campuses, having jobs and families, or often returning to school after a hiatus for work or family. We require our students to complete two semesters of first-year composition but do not offer the courses ourselves. Most have taken them at ASU Main or at the community colleges, and often considerable time has elapsed since they took composition courses or did any academic writing. Many of our students need help with their writing, and help in this area will contribute to improved retention.

Faculty Interest. Because we are an upper-division and graduate campus, we do not have large lower-division courses whose high enrollments discourage faculty from using writing. Our average class size is about 25, and our faculty are eager to use writing in their graduate and undergraduate classes and are, in fact, doing so. Writing across the curriculum exists de facto at ASU West but exhibits the two common problems of de facto WAC: the faculty are frustrated with the students' apparent lack of writing ability, and the students' real writing problems are exacerbated by many instructors' traditional and somewhat unimaginative use of writing and by their unrealistic expectations. Our faculty are younger on the whole than one finds at most universities (over 60% are untenured). They are eager and energetic, but they are also comparatively inexperienced as teachers (often having their own graduate and undergraduate writing experience fused in memory).

Administrative Support. There is strong administrative support for writing. The provost who hired me—and was new to the job himself—is very supportive of writing. And, at the same time I showed up as vice provost, someone with a distinguished career in rhetoric and composition (Joe Comprone) was named as dean of our College of Arts and Sciences. We had a happy alignment of administrative planets. One other important administrative circumstance: at ASU West, Student Affairs is part of Academic Affairs, run by a dean who is parallel to the academic deans, all of whom report to Academic Affairs. Thus, the turf wars between Academic Affairs and Student Affairs occur less frequently at West than at places where Student Affairs is a separate vice provostial or vice-presidential area.

Resources. ASU West has been fortunate to have strong support from local legislators who recognized that a new campus like a new store needs to be front loaded: stocked and staffed *before* the customers show up. The campus has been kept off the state formula and funded according to a sensible and generous start-up plan. While our resources are not unlimited, we have resources available to address our instructional needs and, in this case, to develop writing as an integral part of our curriculum. We are not in the position of many mature universities where a new program can be established only at the expense of existing programs.

We were tempted to create an upper division writing requirement, since we have no control over our students' writing preparation. But we quickly realized that this was retrograde thinking. First, the teaching of writing usually winds up in required writing courses because no one else is doing it. At West campus, we had faculty doing writing in the disciplines, lots of it. Creating a writing requirement might cause them to give up ownership of writing. Moreover, a junior writing requirement would not serve our graduate students, who also struggle with their writing. Finally, we knew that a required writing course would, as enrollments grew, lure us into relying increasingly on graduate students and part-timers for instruction. In the end, we would wind up recreating a composition program, with all of a typical program's theoretical problems and practical vices.

Clearly, we were an ideal site for a writing across the curriculum program with two major features: (1) a seasoned WAC director who could channel the faculty's willingness to use writing into constructive approaches conducive to improving writing and enhancing learning; and (2) a Writing Center (run by the WAC director) where any member of the ASU West community could get assistance with their writing.

Making this decision was easy. Trite but true, the devil is in the details. For example, where would we put the WAC director and Writing

Center administratively? Often, they are in English departments or in colleges of arts and sciences. We don't have an English department as such, and the branch campus era had been hard on our College of Arts and Sciences. Because Business and Education had focused missions, they were reasonably mature programs by the time we achieved NCA accreditation. In fact, one year after NCA accreditation, our Business programs received AACSB accreditation. Focus was also an advantage for the programs in our College of Human Services (Recreation, Administration of Justice, Social Work, and Communication). Both Recreation and Social Work received professional accreditation within 2 years of campus NCA accreditation. However, because of enrollment-driven and opportunistic hiring, West campus Arts and Sciences faculty had been spread thinly over the programs in the Main campus's enormous College of Liberal Arts and Sciences. We had faculty in many disciplines, but little depth anywhere. In order to offer majors that students could complete wholly at West, the Arts and Sciences faculty early on proposed and developed five interesting interdisciplinary majors—making a virtue of necessity and establishing interdisciplinarity as a fundamental value of the campus. The faculty of American Studies, mostly historians by training and responsible for degrees in American Studies, English, History, and Spanish, were planning to "do something" in writing. But they have one rhetoric and composition specialist, very able and dedicated but also untenured and facing tenure and promotion standards developed by historians. In fact, the unit really did not have the resources to devote to this project, and they had no one who could take an institutional perspective on writing. The dean and I agreed that if American Studies conducted the search for a WAC director, we might get something quite different from what we needed.

Fortunately, we were then reshaping an academic unit—part of the original campus plan— called "Interunit Programs." The only existing interunit program was Women's Studies, but other programs, for example, one in Southwestern Studies, had been planned but abandoned. Women's Studies faculty were feeling vulnerable, yet they were not eager to be assigned to a college and lose their "campus" mission. We decided to rename "Interunit Programs" the "Division of Collaborative Programs." It would be home for departments like Women's Studies that did not want to be owned by one college. It would also be an "incubator" for multidisciplinary programs that cut across college boundaries, like gerontology, ethnic studies, and transnational studies. And it would house academic support programs like the Writing Center and—next year—the Statistics Center. Collaborative Programs does not have a dean; the Vice Provost for Academic Programs supervises the division. This looks strange on an organization chart, but we now have an administrative structure (or maybe a gap in the administrative structure) that creates a place for planning and developing programs that go beyond the boundaries of a single college—formal, institutionally sanctioned, interunit collaboration space.

The WAC director and the Writing Center became part of the Division of Collaborative Programs, with campus responsibilities and mission and a reporting line to a campus-level rather than a college-level administrator. We were sending the message that writing is a campus-wide concern that has support at the highest administrative levels. With this structure in mind, we then set about to hire a WAC director—a senior appointment (with tenure) for an experienced WAC person broadly knowledgeable about discourse in the disciplines and able to talk to people about writing in their own disciplines. The job involved establishing and managing a comprehensive writing center, training tutors, working with faculty on effective strategies for using writing in different disciplines, and generally pursuing whatever opportunities the director found for improving writing. The person also had to have a high tolerance for ambiguity, reckless abandon, and ungrounded confidence that we would make it all work out right.

Using the Arizona climate and an interesting opportunity as bait, we found a person with just the right qualifications and personality living in a very cold and snowy place and eager enough for warmth to leave there in March and start the job a few months early. Once he agreed to join us, things got even more interesting.

No matter how big or small a campus is, it has problems with horizontal communication. Information moves up and down administrative silos easily, but it never seems to move across—which may be a strong argument for management by walking around. As I walked the campus looking for good space for the Writing Center and the director's office, I found a bunch of mom and pop tutoring stores operating innocent of or indifferent to one another's existence. American Studies was, in fact, devoting its scarce resources to running a small writing center, sometimes, in a classroom somewhere, open to anyone who could find it. Multicultural Student Services in Student Affairs had combined some of its own resources with a renewable grant from the state to operate a tutoring center available only to minority students. Then I learned that DOE had awarded us a $175,000 TRIO grant to set up a Student Support Services Program—with a substantial writing and math tutoring components—to serve economically disadvantaged students. The TRIO project required substantial contributions of ASU West resources as well. And now Academic Affairs was committed to a Writing Center of yet another sort—by process of elimination—to serve rich anglo students. These projects were scattered all over the campus, all over the org charts, and all over the budget book.

Imagine the entry in the student handbook to direct students to help
with writing. "Need help with your writing? If you're minority and poor,
go to x, y, or z. If you're just minority, go to y or z. If you're just poor, go
to x or z. If you're anglo and rich, go to z only." This is what happens when
types of funding rather than the needs of students drive planning (or lack
of planning). This is not student friendly; it is not a good use of resources;
and it make no sense for a new campus, especially, to diffuse its efforts in
this manner. Administrators are paid the big bucks to fix stuff like this,
and we agreed that it was time to earn our money.

We set some important goals:

1. Insofar as possible, all tutorial services on campus should
be centralized in an attractive, welcoming, and convenient location.

2. All students should have access to the services offered. The
administrative and budgetary complexities of the center should
be transparent to students.

3. The integrity of restricted funds (external grants) must be
preserved and their use satisfactorily accounted for.

4. We had to find a way for the unit to function administratively.

This has been a challenging project so far, and it's still under
construction. The WAC director arrived in March of 1994, and, because
tact, good nature, and political astuteness are among his many good
qualities, he took the point in combining all these initiatives—backed by
an institutional will to make it work. We identified a substantial area in the
University Center that could be remodeled to provide ample tutorial
space for many years to come and sufficient office space for various
program coordinators, including the Writing Center director. There was
some conflict over the space since part of it was already occupied by the
Minority Student Services tutorial program. They would continue to use
the space, but in moving walls, we "took" the space from Minority
Student Services and walled it in with the Writing Center. Some good
negotiating and bridge-building along with a gentle reminder that "all
space belongs to the provost" (and a back door connected to Multicultural
Student Services offices) brought the space issue to closure.

There was a clash of philosophies about what tutorial space should
be. Some of us favored an open and airy feel, with high visibility from the
hallway, a pod of computers for group activities, a couple of free-standing
work stations for word processing, and big round tables for tutoring
individuals or groups. Other parties involved had been tutoring in carrels
and wanted to continue to do so. We could not resolve this one. Thus, a
student coming in the single entrance now sees the open writing tutoring

area to the left and the dark, labyrinthine tutoring carrels to the right. Virtually all students prefer the open space and automatically move toward it, causing some competition for the tables at peak times. The carrels will probably disappear next year when we put in some glass walls and more windows to open the place up and to get the students in the center visually before they are in it physically. The students have spoken.

This common facility—funded out of different pockets and combining people with ties to different units—needed to share some staff and office machines simply for efficiency's sake. Different campuses might handle these matters differently, depending on the local circumstances. On our campus, the Writing Center budget (developed in Academic Affairs) includes the director's secretary, peer writing tutors, and student employees who serve at the reception desk. Student Affairs bought the copy machine, and Academic Affairs pays the annual service contract. Academic Affairs bought the FAX, and we used year-end money (i.e., provost's money) to set up the computers and other technology (which are now part of a campus-wide maintenance and replacement strategic plan). All parties contribute to supplies and phones, since all grants included funds for these purposes. We discovered that any tutor or counselor whose salary came 100% from TRIO funds could serve only TRIO eligible students. Since this didn't serve our purposes, we shifted 25% of the salaries of TRIO people who worked directly with students to ASU Funds and shifted TRIO funds to other purposes in the grant. Unanticipated bits and pieces of this sort keep coming up, but we are managing to deal with them as we go. We want the students to see the duck swimming gracefully across the water, not the mad churning underneath. That's *our* problem, not theirs.

We now offer our students an attractive and friendly place where they can go to get help with their academic work. (The Writing Center director has insisted, quite properly, on allowing food and drink in the center; this irritates maintenance people in principle, but they have as yet no actual damage to point to.) We are promoting the center as a place that students can go without feeling stigmatized somehow or without doing a personal inventory of their race, class, gender, or socio-economic status to figure out where to go. When they come in the first time, we ask them to register, and we get the information we need to allocate them to the appropriate funding source, depending upon the restrictions imposed. But they can get help from anyone available. Generally speaking, we are doing a good job of fund accounting; it doesn't hurt that we have one funding source—Academic Affairs—that is unrestricted (not unlimited).

We haven't done anything about our fourth goal —the one having to do with administrative functioning. The Center functions collaboratively, by default. Three directors have offices there: the Director of Writing Across the Curriculum, who supervises and trains almost all of the writing tutors and uses the Center as the base for his WAC operations; the Director of the TRIO grant program—which includes math tutoring, career counseling, personal counseling, and support for disabled students; and the Coordinator of the state-funded tutoring program for minorities. Each administrator has unique responsibilities as well as common responsibilities in the Center. There is no "super-director"—one of these directors elevated over the others or another director over them all. The reporting lines of all directors are different. The Writing Center director reports directly to Academic Affairs. The other two directors report directly to different Student Affairs administrators and through them to Academic Affairs. Their shared job is to make this creature work according to the goals that have guided its development, to provide the highest possible quality of service to students, to resolve conflicts among themselves. It seems to be working.

E pluribus unum? We've probably been about as successful at this as the United States. Not quite a melting pot; more of a hearty soup. The Writing Center project gave us the opening to bring several maverick supplementary instructional projects together into an attractive and highly visible central facility where all students know that they can get academic assistance. The administrative and budgetary complexity of the Center is totally invisible to students, and students and faculty are coming to view the Center as a resource like the library or the computer center—not like a first-aid station or as a place where you go only if there is something wrong with you. This experiment would be a success if this is all we accomplished. But we've accomplished more. As these programs have operated side by side (more in a matrix than a hierarchy), they have negotiated solutions to problems and have pursued opportunities for collaboration and shared responsibility. The Writing Center has absorbed totally the writing tutoring we committed to in the TRIO proposal and is working with Multicultural Student Services on training and supervising writing tutors. The scope of the Center is enhanced by the combined presence of all of these programs, providing a base for a full learning center. We are able to get more mileage out of limited budgets, offering extended hours and a broader range of services. Also, since grant money tends—especially nowadays—to run out, it will be easier for us to absorb the cost of this more efficient centralized operation.

The Writing Center, of course, is not just a "site" with a mission in supplementary instruction, nor is the Director only the administrator of the site. The Center is also part of an academic unit, the Division of Collaborative Programs, and the Director is a faculty member who has responsibilities for faculty development in WAC and the option of teaching courses. The Writing Center is destined to become the hub for a multidisciplinary program in rhetoric and writing. As a small campus, we can afford a *program* in Rhetoric and Writing only by creating it in Collaborative Programs, by combining courses from curricula campus wide with a small methodological core, first, into a certificate, then a minor, and ultimately a major. This strategy will promote attention to writing and communication issues in courses across the campus, something that is part of our institutional mission. Students in all majors will get substantial writing experience, while students with a special interest in rhetoric and writing can assemble a multidisciplinary concentration. This is a model we will follow also with ethnic studies, transnational studies, and gerontology.

This whole project remains in process, and it is not problem free. For example, no one seems to be sure whether the Writing Center director works for Student Affairs or Academic Affairs; they are uncertain about his title; the current location of his tenure is interesting; and they don't know where to put him in the campus phone book. These are outcroppings of deeper issues, but they are only issues if we think about these matters in conventional ways. Generally, we are pleased with how things are going so far:

1. We have a Writing Center with a solid footprint in the continuation budget. Because of its affiliation with Academic Affairs, it is a much stronger player in the annual budget derby than it would be as a budget item buried in a college or department budget.

2. It is clear that the Writing Center has a campus mission and that the director is free to move across college boundaries.

3. The Writing Center provided us the occasion to pull together maverick academic support initiatives into a centralized, cost effective, and efficient comprehensive learning center.

4. We have improved our service to students by simplifying access, de-stigmatizing academic support, increasing the quality of our support programs, and increasing student persistence or retention in a "writing rich" curriculum.

5. We have established a base for a multidisciplinary writing program in the future.

We'll see where it goes from here.

The particular circumstances at ASU West have been especially propitious for a project of this sort. ASU West is a new campus still building its academic profile and culture. And, in this case, the Writing Center initiative came from central administration rather than being brought to central administration. However, there is no better place to look for the values of central administrators than in the projects that they (OK, we) propose or support. The "quality" movement has left its mark on administrators, and we tend to value projects that are student centered. We like projects that encourage retention, since losing students is expensive and state legislators are on our case. We *have* to be concerned about costs. We favor solutions over problems. We like proposals that reflect an understanding of the institution at large. We also like projects that help to overcome the vertical organization of the institution, reduce duplication, and allow for recombinations of existing resources. It would make sense for proponents of writing centers to build alliances with other academic support programs and come to central administration with a comprehensive proposal. And so on. I would not pretend to be sufficiently self-aware to identify all of the values and assumptions in this project, but I do know that I am not a whole lot different from other administrators. Thus, readers are encouraged to do their own searches of this project for paths to administrative hearts (yes) and to do their best.

The Dark Side of the Helping Personality: Student Dependency and the Potential for Tutor Burnout

Steve Sherwood
Texas Christian University

Most of us can recall times when we let our urge to help a student lead us astray. My own most recent case was Lisa, who came to the writing center with a paper on Roman religion. She'd written ten pages with no clear thesis beyond her assumption that the Romans of 450 BC were Christian. With all the kindness I could muster, I explained the meaning of "BC."

She gave me a shattered look. "You mean I'm going to have to redo the whole thing?"

I probably should have said yes and sent her straight to the library. But she threw herself on my mercy, and out of sympathy (or perhaps an exaggerated sense of duty) I let her. During the next hour, which I ought to have spent grading papers, I explained the Roman pantheon, helped her formulate a thesis, devised a workable essay structure, and showed her how to salvage some of the work she'd already done. She claimed the university library had no books on ancient Rome, so I Xeroxed relevant material from my bookshelf, then accessed the library catalog to find several listings on the topic, which I gave her. While I was doing this, she asked if I thought we might finish in time for her sorority meeting. When she left, Lisa smiled gratefully, said she'd be back often, and promised to tell all her friends to come see me, to which I reacted with a blend of emotions—chiefly horror.

At the time, my reaction surprised me. Like most of us, I work in a writing center because it suits my personality. Helping students blossom as writers gives me joy, a sense of purpose, a chance to gratify my altruistic urges. Toiling over essays until my vision blurs fits neatly into my family's Midwestern work ethic, which lists travail under cardinal virtues. After a long afternoon of tutoring, I might rail about the inequities of academic life or glare at a colleague who bitches about having no time to write but seldom misses a happy hour. Most often, though, I'll go home feeling good about myself on a fundamental level. After all, I belong to a profession whose central aim—like that of ministers or doctors—is to help others. I've come to realize, however, that the altruism that forms a key part of the tutor's helping personality has a dark side. Some of us carry too far our willingness to sacrifice time, energy, even cherished ideals for our students. Michael J. Mahoney alludes to psychotherapists, but he could as easily refer to tutors in saying,

> Regrettably, some practitioners appear to derive satisfaction from what Fromm has termed *neurotic unselfishness,* an attribute they often regard with pride as if it were a redeeming character trait.... such individuals may go to great lengths to live a lifestyle of constant self-sacrifice and extensive public (or client) service .... living their life "entirely for others" .... (355-56, emphasis in original)

We're quite right to take pride in working hard to help students, but we should be careful not to fall prey to our own good intentions. For when altruism degrades into neurotic unselfishness, it can lead to student dependency and tutor burnout. It can also lead those we serve (our students, colleagues, and administrators) to take our services for granted.

The term *altruism* carries mostly good connotations, and I certainly wouldn't suggest that writing centers would be better off if tutors were selfish scoundrels. Rather, the traits of the altruist read like a shopping list for the ideal tutor. Among other qualities, altruists tend to be empathic, sensitive, self-sacrificing, hardworking, and dedicated to upholding ethical standards. Good tutors share with altruists what psychologist Peter Salovey calls *emotional intelligence,* "a set of skills concerning the appropriate recognition of emotions in the self and others and the use of emotional information to solve problems and motivate others" (Salovey et al. 228). Obviously we need emotionally intelligent tutors who can empathize well enough to effectively teach diverse student writers. This kind of altruism is essential to good tutoring, letting us shape our students in positive ways.

But a deeper link runs between altruism and tutoring. By tending to students' needs, we express our most cherished values and, in the process, shape ourselves. Historian Joseph Amato says, "The sympathy we extend to one another establishes our humanity" (196). Psychologists suggest that the biggest rewards for altruistic behavior come from "establishing one's self-identity, confirming one's notion of the sort of person one sees oneself to be, and expressing the values appropriate to this self-concept" (Katz and Kahn, qtd. in Clary and Snyder 141). The urge to define the self through work, they argue, motivates the helping personality far more potently than public recognition or profit (141).

And it would have to in most writing centers, where tutors work not simply for six-figure salaries, but for such idealistic notions as wanting to help people, or in my case wanting to do penance for the agony I caused my own writing teachers. If our sacrifice of eyesight and earning potential boosts our sense of self-identity and self-esteem, what could be wrong with that?

The answer is nothing, I suppose, as long we temper our altruistic urges with good sense. This is a challenge for any dedicated tutor, but especially for the neurotically unselfish, to whom no tutorial is too long, no task too big, no budget too small. Found in many writing centers, they reveal themselves by the inner glow on their weary faces. In hopes of making self-diagnosis easier for the neurotically unselfish among us, I've identified a number of symptoms. Such tutors, for example,

- Have never met a student they couldn't help.
- Are unable to resist rescuing a student from the fruits of mental laziness or (sometimes flawed) creative vision.
- Often care more about a student's paper than the student does, and end up doing most of the work.
- Feel intense misgivings at sending a student away without radically marking up a paper.
- Take pleasure from what other reasonably selfless tutors would characterize as dull, painful, unduly rigorous, or too frequent contact with students.
- Have a large following of fiercely loyal but abjectly dependent students willing to wait for hours rather than accept another tutor's help.
- Routinely stay late or continue tutorials outside the writing center.
- See the refusal to take breaks as somehow virtuous.
- Would be willing, if asked, to continue working for little (or no) pay.

In analyzing such behavior, a psychologist might read into it the unconscious hope that giving painstaking attention to student writing qualifies a tutor for sainthood. And quite possibly it should. In any case, a team of researchers claims one common way of becoming a martyr is to suffer "great pain or misery for a long time" (Weiner and Weiner 9), and depending on the location this might apply to writing center work. But I'm less interested in pegging neurotically unselfish tutors as closet martyrs than in exploring the unintended consequences of their behavior, one of which is student dependency.

Not all dependency is harmful, of course, especially the symbiotic sort. Psychologist Albert Memmi says, "Accepting a relative dependence can be an indication of confidence in oneself .... "(150). Some students bring to the center a strong sense of autonomy and faith in their ability. They may rely on us to identify inconsistencies of voice or logic, but they plan to iron out such wrinkles themselves and resent a tutor's attempt to "correct" a paper. Others need us to help them generate ideas, calm their fears, and set them back on the right road (or show them they never left it). This level of dependency usually strikes me as healthy—doubly so when the student is as creatively engaged during a session as I.

Dependency becomes unhealthy when a student leans too heavily on a tutor and the tutor accepts the burden. My most troublesome case of this happened early in my career, when I was a graduate assistant in a new writing center. A woman I'd worked with for months, during which she weathered a number of personal crises, came in looking flustered. In a fragile tone of voice, she said,

> "They told me at the English department you're not coming back next year."
> When I nodded, tears formed in her eyes. "You can't leave."
> "I'm graduating," I said. "And I've taken a job at Montana State."
> "Well, what am *I* supposed to do?" she asked.

I suggested she work with another tutor; she wondered aloud about her chances of transferring to Montana State. All of which drove home that by intervening too directly, not simply as advisor but as indispensable rescuer and benefactor, I'd failed her. For even given with good intentions, too much help stunts a student's intellectual growth, thwarting what should be our primary goal. As Mahoney says, "Optimal helping encourages the empowerment of the individual as the primary agent of choice and action in his or her own life" (270). B.F. Skinner seconds this, using the analogy of a parent who ties a boy's shoe rather than taking the time to teach him how to tie it himself. He adds, "By giving too much help we postpone the acquisition of effective behavior and perpetuate the need for help" (251). We seldom empower students by proofing papers or doing their thinking (or writing) for them. Such efforts reap short-term benefits—gratification for us and higher grades for them—but at the cost of long-term deficits in student confidence and self-efficacy.

Meanwhile, knowing who really did the work, our students fall deeper into dependency, demanding still more of our time and emotional support. Such relationships nearly always end in failure and frustration,

Memmi says, because "the dependent's expectations are so high that she is bound to be disappointed, and the rest follows: disappointment leads to irritation, and irritation to malevolence .... " (50). The student who threatened to follow me to Montana State had needs that went beyond the realm of writing and beyond my strict obligation, as a tutor, to satisfy. One day, she might say, "You're the only one at this university who talks to me like a person." The next, she might tearfully accuse me of disliking her. The stress of such encounters takes a toll, especially as dependents grow in number and intensity of need. To satisfy the snowballing demands of even one dependent, much less all, a tutor would need a "benevolence ... that is perfect in intention and totally adequate" (Memmi 45), which it can never be. And so, unable to succeed despite heroic effort, the neurotically unselfish tutor eventually suffers from exhaustion and disillusionment. In plainer words, he or she burns out.

According to psychologist Ayala Pines, burnout results from "intense involvement with people over long periods of time in situations that are emotionally demanding" (455). Professional helpers like our neurotic tutors, who "started out being the most idealistic and caring" (455) and who "set high work goals for themselves, their recipients, and for the organization" (464), are the most susceptible to burnout. Pines suggests this is because the traits that make such people especially effective helpers also "make them more sensitive to the emotional pressures inherent in their work" (464). Burnout can reduce dedicated, capable professionals to a state "marked by physical depletion and chronic fatigue, by feelings of hopelessness and helplessness, and by the development of negative self-concept and negative attitudes toward work, life, and other people" (455). In extreme instances, Pines says, helpers who suffer from burnout "typically lose concern for their clients" and "may come to treat their clients in detached and even dehumanized ways" (455).

The image of a writing center staffed by a pack of burnout cases may make us shudder, but if we're honest, most of us will admit to flirting with the syndrome. On a bad day, usually when I'm trying to meet a deadline, I've been known to mutter to the secretary about being too accessible or threaten to go berserk if forced to read another paper on the Brady Bill. Fortunately, these lapses are temporary, and I haven't yet sunk so low as to treat a student in a detached or dehumanized way, but the sour periods worry me, make me wonder if it's time to move on. Apparently, and I take some small comfort from this, such doubts are merely another aspect of burnout. As Pines says, burned out helpers sometimes

> quit their field altogether and make a career change to a field that does not involve stressful work with people. Some professionals climb the administrative ladder as a way of avoiding direct client

contact; others remain in their positions as 'dead wood' doing just enough not to get fired. In all cases burnout represents a great loss for the individual, the organization, and society as a whole. (455)

If dependency and burnout aren't worrisome enough, we must also examine the effects of neurotic unselfishness on our profession as a whole. We often work longer hours for less pay than most academics, and many of us run our operations on skimpy budgets. Speaking of writing center folk, Richard Leahy has said, "'If they have to, they'll try to provide service in some way on practically no budget at all'" (qtd. in Sherwood 8). In fact, Katya Amato had to do just that at Portland State when the administration cut her personnel budget. For a year Amato continued to give service with unpaid tutors, what she called her "twenty-five points of light" (7). But as she says of the selfless efforts of her volunteers and of her own heartbreaking attempt to save her center by getting along without funding (which ultimately ended when she resigned),

sometimes I wonder whether we should hold on, whether we should cooperate in our own exploitation. I know why we do it—our damned social consciences, our respect and affection for students ... but making do cannot enhance our professional standing and can ultimately cost all of us our jobs, can wipe out our field. (7)

After all, administrators may well ask why their university is paying for a service that tutors elsewhere are willing to provide free of charge. As Amato says, "If we can make bricks without straw, then why should the administration give us any straw at all?" (7). Experience tells us that universities value most highly the programs and employees in which they have invested the most money. The same basic principle applies to sacrifices tutors make for students during tutorials. Thomas Paine observed, "What we obtain too cheap, we esteem too lightly." Perhaps, then, we can forgive students who take our "free" advice and hard work for granted—especially when we place so little value on our time that we willingly contribute more to tutorials, and too often to papers, than the students do.

In view of this, we probably ought to do what we can to defend ourselves from the "unintended consequences of our benevolence" (Marcus 66). Beyond refusing to volunteer our services, we can temper our neurotic unselfishness by practicing a bit of enlightened self-interest. I say *enlightened* because by protecting ourselves from the effects of unhealthy dependency and burnout, we protect our students, too.

Perhaps we should begin by approaching tutorials with what Pines calls *detached concern* (470), balancing our empathic regard for a student with careful objectivity toward his or her writing problems. This fits nicely into the "less is more" philosophy Jeff Brooks calls minimalist tutoring. Brooks says, "We need to make the student the primary agent in the writing center session" (2). Among other things, he suggests we have students read papers aloud, detecting any errors themselves, and that we issue continual reminders about who owns the paper (3-4). We can also warn students to be skeptical because we make mistakes, freely admit when we can't help them, even refuse them certain services. By insisting they do what they can for themselves (for instance, teaching them how to fix a comma splice instead of fixing it for them), we put their long-term growth ahead of short-term gains, fostering writers who have a sense of self-efficacy and who may someday learn to rely on their own resources.

Doing so automatically lessens our chances of succumbing to burnout. But we can do still more by improving job conditions in writing centers. Pines cites studies that show that a "lack of positive work features such as money, significance, growth, autonomy, and supportive social networks was significantly correlated with burnout" (461). Decent salaries and stock option plans for tutors would be nice. In any case, since profit is only a secondary motivation for neurotically unselfish tutors, who are the most susceptible to burnout, we might find it more effective to address the job's other features. For example, Pines says,

> Enlightened organizations can help prevent burnout by changing conditions in the helping environment, such as maintaining a manageable staff-client ratio, enabling flexibility in client selection, permitting time out, encouraging lateral job changes, and limiting involvement in stressful client contact. (471)

One can easily imagine the issues of race, nationality, gender, and social bias raised by letting tutors select the type students they will or will not assist. But Pines's other suggestions might work in writing centers committed to giving good service while sustaining a high level of professionalism. By staffing the center adequately, letting overwrought tutors take short breaks (even if this means making students wait), sharing an especially difficult student among several tutors, and giving one another emotional support (face-to-face or via WCENTER), we create a collaborative space conducive to the productive, dignified exchange of ideas, within which student confidence and skills can flourish.

In doing so, perhaps we can lay to rest the image of writing center as basement broom closet: desperate students lined up outside, while inside a well-meaning tutor/martyr rescues papers, feeling virtuous as he or she nurtures dependency and moves inexorably toward the brink of burnout. For our students' sake and our own, we must strike a workable balance between altruism and neurotic unselfishness. And as each of us wrestles with our "damned social conscience[s]" (K. Amato 7) in an attempt to do so, it might help to remember that "Limiting our sympathy is the act of simple recognition that our hearts are not infinite" (J. Amato 196).

Works Cited

Amato, Joseph Anthony, II. *Guilt and Gratitude: A Study of the Origins of Contemporary Conscience*. Westport: Greenwood, 1982.

Amato, Katya. "Making Bricks Without Straw: The Fate of One Writing Center." *Writing Lab Newsletter* 17.10 (1993): 4-7.

Brooks, Jeff. "Minimalist Tutoring: Making the Student Do All the Work." *Writing Lab Newsletter* 15.6 (1991): 1-4.

Clary, E. Gil, and Mark Snyder. "A Functional Analysis of Altruism and Prosocial Behavior: The Case of Volunteerism." *Prosocial Behavior*. Ed. Margaret S. Clark. Newbury Park: Sage, 1991. 119-48.

Mahoney, Michael J. *Human Change Processes: The Scientific Foundations of Psychotherapy*. New York: HarperCollins, 1991.

Marcus, Steven. "Their Brothers' Keepers: An Episode from English History." *Doing Good: The Limits of Benevolence*. Ed. Willard Gaylin, Ira Glasser, Steven Marcus, and David J. Rothman. New York: Pantheon, 1978. 67-96.

Memmi, Albert. *Dependence: A Sketch for a Portrait of the Dependent*. Trans. Philip A. Facey. Boston: Beacon, 1984. Trans. of *La Dépendance*. 1979.

Pines, Ayala. "Helpers' Motivation and the Burnout Syndrome." *Basic Processes in Helping Relationships*. Ed. Thomas Ashby Wills. New York: Academic, 1982. 453-75.

Salovey, Peter, John D. Mayer, and David L. Rosenhan. "Mood and Helping: Mood as a Motivator of Helping and Helping as a Regulator of Mood." *Prosocial Behavior*. Ed. Margaret S. Clark. Newbury Park: Sage, 1991. 215-37.

Sherwood, Steve. "How to Survive the Hard Times." Writing *Lab Newsletter* 17.10 (1993): 4-8.

Skinner, B.F. "The Ethics of Helping People." *Altruism, Sympathy, and Helping: Psychological and Sociological Principles*. Ed. Lauren Wispé. New York: Academic, 1978. 249-62.

Weiner, Eugene, and Anita Weiner. *The Martyr's Conviction*. Atlanta: Scholars, 1990.

Must We Always Grin and Bear It?

Wangeci JoAnne Karuri
Coe College

Among the thousands of papers that pass through the Coe Writing Center each year, it is inevitable that our staff members (all undergraduates)[1] must occasionally handle papers with offensive content or ideology. A good example is evident in the opening sentences of a paper on racism that an African-American student handed to a white writing consultant:

Racism is not a world problem. It is not a human problem. In fact, racism is a white problem. Whites are the only people in the world capable of having this mental disorder.

While the confrontational tone of this paper may not be encountered every day, when such a paper does appear, staff members need a game-plan for preventing "unproductive" conferences.

Uncomfortable situations created by such papers are not unique to writing centers; instructors, too, are inevitably faced with objectionable papers. Their approach, however, may differ from the writing consultant's because their function and goals are different. Instructors have a responsibility to question a student's ideas and the validity of conclusions. Many would argue that this responsibility does not extend to the writing center. Faculty and administration expect the writing center to deal with the more literal aspects of writing, such as sentence structure, development and clarity of ideas, style, and organization. Amending the ideas in student compositions is not usually considered a writing center prerogative. However, since the writing center's goal is to help writers effectively present ideas, should we simply ignore the disturbing or repulsive elements in these texts? How do we reconcile our professional duties to student writers with our need to defend personal beliefs and values?

It may be useful to give an illustration of practical situations that our writing center staff members have recently encountered. The papers described, visiting issues of racism, violence, and sexuality, were brought into the Coe Writing Center in the 1993-94 school year. The issues in these papers may not seem objectionable to every individual, but the consultants involved were disturbed to the extent that they felt crippled in their ability to conduct the conferences professionally and objectively. Deeply dissatisfied with these encounters, the consultants discussed their experiences at the weekly staff meetings.

A senior, for example, wrote a paper apparently describing the initiation rites of his fraternity. He spared no details in his seven-page paper, graphically depicting practices he seemed to condone. Many of the described acts qualified as illegal hazing and included shocking acts of violence:

> Hell week was the week that the [fraternity] members were unusually cruel to potential members [scum] to weed out the weaker ones. They had to perform a variety of tasks such as lying naked on top of one another, or having a circle of naked scum with each one of them having one thumb in his mouth and the other placed in the rectum of the scum in front of him with threats by the members of having to switch thumbs at any given moment .... Swats were given by the pledge fathers to their respective sons in the form of a wooden paddle about a foot wide and three to four foot long. These swats were given to the bare-assed scum who was bent over a chair .... the fathers would swing in a baseball stance which usually resulted in deep bruises.

Another conference involved a student writer's response to National Coming-Out Day when a student organization involved in issues of sexual diversity chalked the campus sidewalks with slogans in an attempt to combat homophobia:

> Homosexuals have the right to live as they wish. If two men want to have a relationship, fine .... However they don't have to boast about it. A man and a woman don't brag about being heterosexual, therefore, neither should homosexuals. Just because a person is homosexual does not mean they should get any kind of special treatment.

In these three cases consultants encountered material they found so offensive that their instinct was to terminate each conference. They were unprepared to deal with such conference situations. But what should they have done? When writing center consultants assist writers with such papers, must we, indeed, grin and bear it?

The staff's discussions of this dilemma initially revolved around two attitudes for handling objectionable manuscripts: avoidance or confrontation. Neither approach required feigning agreement with the writer, but each comes with its own set of difficulties. The following list gives a breakdown of the two general strategies (confrontation and avoidance) and outlines three levels of confrontation hypothesized in staff discussions:

Confrontation

Direct:

- Admit personal opposition to the writer's argument/discussion.
- Take issue with the morality of the paper.

Indirect:

- Play the devil's advocate and ask for the writer's responses to possible counter arguments.
- Ask the writer to reassert the paper's main points, and question points as they are raised.

Subtle:

- Ask questions of tone, rhetorical goals, and possible audience responses.
- Ask about differing or opposing viewpoints.
- Use humor for questioning a paper's ideas, tone, etc.

Avoidance

- Ignore the contents. Focus on the technical aspects, such as sentence structure, punctuation, and organization.

- Refrain from expressing a personal opinion on the matter.

- Ask if the student would prefer meeting with a different consultant.

Several staff members advocated an avoidance strategy so they would not have to acknowledge their disagreement or try to change the writer's position. They counseled the staff to focus on grammatical issues and ignore the paper's content. A second contingent of staff members argued that it was their responsibility to deal with the content of a paper. Our Writing Center Handbook, which establishes fundamental principles for our consulting, embraces confrontation as a natural result of some conferences. In describing our program as a "talking center," the Handbook recommends that we work with a relative lack of censorship, encouraging open-mindedness in both ourselves and in student writers. Our responsibility to writers is analogous to the baking process. Ideas are like bread dough, and a writing center should help in the mixing and kneading process. Just as no amount of baking will compensate for relying on poor ingredients, no amount of technical and syntactic work will improve a paper based on shallow, ill-conceived ideas. Avoiding the fundamental content of the papers will consistently result in half-baked products.

Another important consideration should be the student's needs and expectations. There are situations in which a student brings a paper into the center, possibly even to a specific consultant, seeking a dissenting viewpoint. Here is a passage from a writer's logbook, describing the work she did while preparing a paper for a composition class:

> I brought this paper in during a time when I knew Julie was working. I wanted her specifically to read it because I knew she holds very traditional views on a lot of things. I'm not sure if I hoped that she would convince me out of my newly acquired ideas, or if I thought she would be able to strengthen my paper by bringing up opposing view points.

In this case, the consultant decided to admit that she disagreed with the writer's position; the student reported positive results:

> I think her disagreement added to my paper. The draft I had brought her was a complete jumble …. After talking with Julie, I realized that I really do believe the argument that surfaced in my paper.

This is a good conference situation to be in. It is satisfying to work with a student who acknowledges an alternative perspective, recognizing this tension as an opportunity to strengthen an argument. Such openness, however, is not always the case. Some students will be defensive about their opinions and may not tolerate what they consider to be an attack. The question then arises: how do we pick or choose whom or what to challenge? Can we work only within certain boundaries?

As the staff explored various strategies for handling these difficult papers, our writing center director recommended we organize a presentation on this issue for the NWCA conference in New Orleans. This project was to be a learning catalyst for us, and we looked forward to sharing our ideas and frustrations with writing center staff members from other institutions and gaining insights from them. In preparation for this presentation, the five staff members involved in this project prepared sample case studies for a small survey, geared at detecting trends among our group and possibly introducing new options for consideration. The case studies we created were based on our own personal experiences and a series of recent articles in *Writing Lab Newsletter* by Michael Pemberton from the University of Illinois at Urbana–Champaign. We modeled the case studies to elicit a wide range of responses, while keeping the situations practical and conceivable. The issues addressed were religion, pornography, racism, and politics.

Even within our small group, there were varying ideas on how to handle a problem conference. Our differences, we hope, reflect a desirable tolerance for diversity among student writers and consultants. Nevertheless, despite our varied tutoring styles, we discovered some commonalties in our thinking. For example, the majority favored adopting indirect or subtle confrontation as a strategy for these conferences. Everyone felt the writer should keep the paper as inoffensive as possible (curbing the use of insulting language, for example) because people who are offended or insulted are rarely people who will be convinced to change their thinking. The consultants should remind their peers that an assault on the reader will usually make it impossible to achieve any positive purpose.

Our research team frequently discussed the importance of determining the writer's purpose and intended audience. This clarification can determine what direction the conference should take, the purpose becoming a gauge for examining language, sources, and arguments. If, for example, the writer of the paper on racism was trying to write a journal-type article for publication on a multi-racial college campus, his opening paragraph would certainly be unsuitable because he is attacking and insulting his audience.

A common recommendation was for consultants either suggesting to the writer that many readers might be offended by the paper or admitting that they were personally disturbed by the paper's content or style. An important factor in taking such an approach, according to the consultants, is to assure the writer that this is a golden opportunity for critical analysis and strengthening of the paper. This reassurance must not be overlooked; otherwise, it may seem as though the consultant is seeking to change the writer's position, which should not be the case.

Several consultants also indicated they would question the writers' sources to ensure that the original authors are correctly quoted and encourage the writers to support their more controversial statements with reliable sources.

As we examined these case study responses and reconsidered our initial staff discussions, it was possible to identify three basic questions that should be considered before acting in the face of offensive (or inoffensive) material. We tried to phrase questions that would apply to virtually any conference situation and, at the same time, highlight the basic concerns we think consultants should have in mind. The first of these was: what are the goals, purposes, and motivations of the people involved? This entails obtaining background information on writers. It would be futile to try to help them reach their goals without being aware of what they want to achieve. The assignment must be established early because it indicates the instructor's expectations. Consultants must assess their own agendas, guaranteeing that the conference does not become an attempt to take over the writer's opinions.

The second consideration was what are the social and ethical consequences of trying to influence a writer's beliefs, feelings, or arguments during the course of a conference? The staff had to decide how invasive we could be in attempting to influence a writer's idea-forming process.

We needed to consider how our attempts to enter this arena would affect our professional and personal ethics. And the final question was what are the consequences of *not* doing so? It may not be our purpose to influence a writer's opinions, but there may be cases in which we are certain that the ideas are morally, or even legally, wrong or inappropriate.

For our presentation at the NWCA conference, we displayed our outline of the confrontation and avoidance strategies, the sample case-studies, a detailed discussion of our three "vital" questions, and copies of the three papers from which the earlier "offensive" quotations were taken. We also handed out a survey to people who attended our presentation. We were able to access a range of people—college instructors, writing center tutors, and writing center administrators from several states and institutions.

We gained valuable information from our discussions with people at the conference and from reading their survey responses (for statistics, see Appendix). Some individuals offered unique options, such as advocating counseling for writers whose ideas were disturbing. Another respondent reminded us that tolerance is the key; that we, too, need to acknowledge that there are two (or more) sides to any issue and simply tolerate the papers. A majority of the sample felt it is the duty of writing center consultants to discuss (but not necessarily debate) a writer's views even if found offensive. The majority also agreed that they would set boundaries for themselves in such a discussion. These boundaries were established according to two primary principles: (1) not taking ownership of a paper (remaining a facilitator rather than a dictator) and (2) avoiding a situation in which the consultant appears to be making a personal attack on the writer. Most indicated they would be willing to challenge a writer's ideas or assumptions regardless of their own position on the controversial issue.

While most respondents in New Orleans claimed that their performance in a conference would be affected if they had objections to the content, only 30% of these thought that the influence would be positive. This evidence would suggest that many writing center personnel are dissatisfied with their ability to handle conferences in which they find the subject matter disturbing. Despite their dissatisfaction, the respondents indicated they would continue to work with the students rather than refer the writer to another consultant. Passing the conference to another staff member was considered unprofessional and not an acceptable solution.

Most respondents acknowledged they had encountered conferences in which they disagreed with the writer's opinions. From the type of issues that they cited as problematic, the "Big Three" were racism, sexism, and homophobia. Other issues raised were creationism, environmentalist doctrines, religious bigotry, and writers becoming too personal. When respondents were questioned on what they thought the major causes of the disagreements were, ideological and cultural differences were most frequently cited. Other reasons given were levels of maturity, educational background, and experience. Respondents to our questionnaire identified several factors that would influence their approach to offensive papers: the strength of the writer's argument, the writer's personality, the consultant's mood, and familiarity with the writer.

One inescapable responsibility in a writing center is helping all writers who come into the center, whether or not their opinions and values appeal to us. We need to evaluate their situation and adopt the best possible strategy for success in each conference. In handling the conference, whether or not it is offensive, we must seek mutual respect between the authors and ourselves. Maintaining this professional relationship remains a critical objective in any writing center conference. In Gail Brendel's discussion of professional intimacy, she describes the "familiar-professional relationship" (11), in which the conversation between the consultant and writer need not move to the personal plane. This emphasis does not mean that the ideas are not addressed. As Brendel explains in her article, based on a series of conferences with one student, the writer "discussed intimate thoughts and apprehensions, all under the broad umbrella of a writing conference ... she felt comfortable with my attitude as a professional because it relieved her from the agonizing decision of what to tell me."

Professionalism, as described by Brendel, refers to that blend of involvement and disinterest that the writing center staff must maintain within conference situations. The consultant is an important part of the game but is not, and cannot assume the role of, a player. The consultant is an umpire; umpires can make calls (observations) to guide the game but can never actually join in the game or direct plays. Professionalism, then,

refers to responsibility, self-control, and detachment. These factors ensure that both parties are in a stable and functional work relationship,
while familiarity inspires a willingness to work without contempt. These
points are key in approaching tendentious conferences in which a consultant is faced with conflicting loyalties: professional obligation versus
personal opinion or belief. It may be tempting to enter into one-on-one
combat with a writer over what the consultant considers to be atrocious
ideas. These unprofessional approaches, however, would not likely yield
any success in a conference situation or otherwise benefit either party.
Personal conflicts may be avoided by the consultant's maintaining a
familiar-personal relationship. As Brendel recounts, this focus would
make it clear that there is only one agenda: "She understood, from my
attitude and objective stance, that everything she told me was to help in
producing a well-written paper."

Our examination of this issue following the NWCA Conference led
us to new terrain. So far, we had been considering only two approaches
to conferencing over offensive material: avoidance and confrontation.
Our further studies on the issue led to a third approach that resolves the
shortcomings of the other two and incorporates the professionalism that
is so important to maintain. Rather than confronting the writer or skirting
around a bothersome issue, the consultant should try to become a
researcher, committed to understanding the context and background of
the writer. John Trimbur describes this as "a process of identifying
differences and locating these differences in relation to one another"
(608). This approach means asking questions aimed at reaching a consensus, based on the consultant's discovering where this writer is coming
from. Trimbur explains that a consensus does not necessitate collective
agreement. Rather, he describes the philosophy of "consensus as
dissensus." He defines this as "reaching a consensus based on collective
explanations of how people differ, where differences came from, and if
they can live and work together with these differences" (610). The
consultant need not agree with the writer, or vice versa, to reach a
consensus. What the consultant needs to do is reach an understanding of
how and why they differ, thus structuring their differences such that they
can work together to strengthen the writer's paper. In a way, it is
"agreeing to disagree," but with an understanding of why there was the
disagreement in the first place.

Behind this concept of delineating differences is the assumption that
our personal backgrounds send unique messages to us. Kenneth A.
Bruffee says, "We all belong to many overlapping, mutually inclusive
communities" that can be "both limiting and liberating." Student writing
is often a mix of these disparate voices, the "vernacular languages of the
communities one belongs to" (qtd. in Trimbur 609). Consultants would

therefore be trying in vain to analyze an individual's opinion if they insisted on seeing things from their own perspective. The key is in trying to comprehend the writer's perspective.

In a recent article in *College Composition and Communication,* Janice Neuleib frankly states that "teaching students whose goals and dreams differ markedly from one's own demands a re-focus of perspective that often shows both our ignorance and our narrow perspectives" (234). We can only see as writers see if we learn to look through *their* eyes. Neuleib describes at length an episode between a student named Kevin and herself. She recounts her frustrations at trying to understand why Kevin had made various grammatical errors in an assigned writing. She admits that her instinct was to charge in, point out the mistakes, and prescribe the corrections. She realized that her "impulse to help [Kevin] came from my assurance that I had the right information about text production and that he was eager to learn from me" (238). This assumption comes easily to any person who holds a strong opinion on an issue. We assume that we have a privileged angle on the situation, and we are eager to "enlighten" others, given the chance.

Neuleib affirms that good conferencing requires decentered teaching, and instructors often fail to decenter; they automatically assume the role of "expert editor"—a counterbalance to the student's role of novice contributor. When conflicts of opinion arise in a conference situation, it becomes tempting for a consultant to assume the superior stance of the know-all. We must keep in mind that we, too, must listen and learn. In resolving her professional relationship with her students, Neuleib reaches a tentative conclusion that applies to writing center consultants as well: "I must listen to a student like Kevin and try to hear and understand why he would want to retain the cultural assumptions that allow him to say confidently that nothing needs to be changed in a passage that looks all wrong to me" (238).

Reevaluating our own three case studies, we discovered that each example verified the wisdom of Neuleib's advice. For example, the student who wrote the paper on racism later revised the version brought to the Center. He began this revised draft by talking about his imprisoned brother. His brother, whom he had wanted so much to admire, was a frequent failure, unable to thrive in a white society. The writer expressed his anger at the destruction of his family by a system in which black people cannot significantly improve their situation. The new passages profoundly modified the impact of the entire paper, transforming it into a discussion in which a white reader's reaction was likely to be more empathic than repulsed. The initial paper can now be seen for what it was: a writer in the process of discovering the paper he was trying to write. This example demonstrates the futility of focusing on sentence-level problems when the fundamental nature of the paper has not yet been defined.

Further discussion of the fraternity paper led to a reconsideration of a passage previously overlooked. The final paragraph of the paper read,

> The issues that were not very thought twice about are now hurting the all-male fraternity. Things such as coed fraternity, sexual harassment, and equal rights are all things that have changed our society in an attempt to put a stop to such crimes and also crush the good old boy network that not only run the schools, towns, cities, and counties, but even the foundation of this country and what it was based on.

Different readers had interpreted this conclusion quite differently. Some thought that by "issues" the writer was referring to the co-ed fraternities, sexual harassment and so forth, meaning that he was condemning these as factors destroying the "good old boy network." However, others understood that the "issues" not well thought out referred to the fraternity's practices. They interpreted the word "crimes" as indicating the writer's condemnation of these terrible acts. The case reveals how important it is to uncover the author's intentions, understanding the intended thesis and how he feels about his subject. The consultant who first read this paper admitted being unaware of the writer's goal in writing the paper; she found it difficult to look beyond the vulgarities. Solely from the text, it is difficult to infer the writer's intentions: his paper was poorly developed, and the stream of errors in phrasing made many of his points ambiguous. But it is necessary for consultants to be aware of possible misinterpretations and to avoid any rush to judgment.

The paper on sexuality became more understandable after discovering some facts about the writer's background. The student was an only child in a conservative, fundamentalist Christian family. She went to a small-town high school and grew up surrounded by strong homophobic sentiments. In her home there was no question about the wickedness of homosexuality. After arriving in a college situation now, she had been exposed to more sexual diversity and liberal thinking and was still in the turbulent process of forming her own opinions about homosexuality. She viewed herself as being more receptive to homosexuals than she ever been before college. For her, the paper she wrote was a liberating step in her battle with lingering homophobia.

In each situation, the consultants needed to see beyond the immediate text, looking outside the margins, into the context and intent of each author. The only option is by engaging in discussion with the student, aimed at reaching the type of consensus described by Trimbur. Reaching this consensus would mean that the writer has, during the discussion, divulged information for explaining the background and intention of the paper, of filling in various narrative or argumentative gaps permeating any piece of writing. The writing consultant can facilitate this sharing, this "filling in" process, by adopting the role of the supportive researcher, seeking to understand rather than to judge. The conference needs to begin not with the consultant helping the student, but with the student helping the consultant to understand the paper—its history, its themes, and its relationship to the author's ideas. The consultant's failure to reach an understanding of the writer's personal story will often signify an unsuccessful conference—and an unsuccessful paper.

Notes

[1]Other writing consultants contributing to this paper include Krislyn Holaday, Dawn Markham, Kim Potts, and Hilary Sloan.

Works Cited

Brendel, Gail. "Professional Intimacy." *Writing Lab Newsletter* 18.2 (1993):11-12.
Neuleib, Janice. "The Friendly Stranger: Twenty-Five Years as 'Other.'" *College Composition and Communication* 43 (1992): 231-43.
Trimbur, John. "Consensus and Difference in Collaborative Learning." *College English* 51 (1989): 602-16.

Appendix

Twenty-six people were surveyed at one of the poster sessions at the NWCA Conference (1994). The following is a tally of their responses to the eight questions we presented to them:

1). When you are in a conference dealing with a paper you find offensive, do you think it is your job to discuss and debate the issue with the author?

50% - YES
23% - NO
27% - discuss, yes; debate, no

2). If you decide to debate issues in the paper, would there be any boundaries you would set for yourself?

60% - YES
4% - NO
27% - N/A

3). Would dealing with an objectionable paper affect your performance in the conference?

62% - YES
38% - NO

4). Would you rather ask another consultant to take a conference dealing with an objectionable paper?

15% - YES
62% - NO
23% - MAYBE

5) a). Do you often disagree with the content of students' papers?

27% - YES
34% - NO
38% - SOMETIMES

b). Do you think this is mostly due to ideological, cultural, or other differences? (please specify)

42% - ideological
34% - cultural
OTHERS: experience, education, maturity level

6). Do you challenge the ideas or assumptions in a paper even when you agree with the writer's argument?

96% - YES
4% - NO

7). What factors would you consider before deciding what to do in a conference when confronted with a paper you find offensive?

69% - writer's personality
80% - subject matter itself
31% - personal mood that day
96% - strength of writer's argument

8). As a writing consultant, have you had experiences of handling difficult conferences due to the subject matter?

46% - YES
54% - NO (Issues: sexism, racism, homophobia, overly personal papers)

Intellectual (Proper)ty in Writing Centers: Retro Texts and Positive Plagiarism

Cynthia Haynes-Burton
University of Texas at Dallas

This is an in/appropriate essay. By that I mean that portions are appropriated, though it is difficult to see where the sutures occur — no footnotes that take up precious space, after all, "Plagiarism® saves time" (Branwyn 30). I play a jargonaut stirring the unexpected in with the expected, creating tentative gestalts with neurologisms, mixing things up by cannibalizing, sampling, plundering, pirating, hijacking, splicing, bootlegging, pilfering, cribbing, and blending. The result is a kind of hyperstack of transgenic objects, ding-a-linguistics, and worm-holes. Donna Haraway suggests that once you go through a serious worm-hole in history, time, and space, you're never the same ("Modest"). I am not suggesting that you will never be the same after you read this essay, but that you are already not the same, you have already moved through the worm-hole. We are living in the time zone of amazing promises (Haraway), moving toward technographic redefinitions of literacy, composition, and collaboration at speeds in which writing is currency in the net.

Writing is achieved in what Haraway calls an "integrated circuit." That is, reading webs of power and information creates new couplings and new coalitions (*Simians* 170). In writing centers, for example, we sit and lounge and pace and think with writers. And with writers we become mixologists—together. But we are also more than that—we are sociotechnologists, looking for the wormholes, like computers, through which contemporary travelers have been dumped out into contemporary worlds where the relation between property and creativity is imploded (Haraway "Modest"). When we tutor writers, we permeate the boundaries of prior published research, conversations, images, found sounds, and 8.5 x 11, one-inch marginalized double-spaced digital pulp.

Writing centers have a crucial stake in analyzing (and engaging in) debates about the "real estate" of composition, "intellectual property." Although academia may flirt with redefining its apparatus for accountability, the front line has held when it comes to teaching research protocols and scholarship conventions "in the trenches." In other words, not much of the debate has filtered through into mainstream composition pedagogy. The writing center, however, has consistently wrestled with the issue of "intellectual property." Unfortunately, writing centers battle a classic double bind: either we are perceived as helping students too much, or not enough. So, we fly low, avoiding the academic radar designed to fix our location and bring us back to base, and back in line. Recent technology allows us to construct new terrains like online writing centers (OWLs) and new communities like text-based multi-user domains (MOOs). Tutors and students traffic uneasily in the stealth landscape between collaboration and appropriation, a region of textual shadows and mis-located meanings, a region of surveillance and the surveilled student subject. Granted, it is not popular to use military metaphors, much less to signal an assault, but to analyze a fortress sometimes you have to tear it down, to dismantle its political and economic walls.

In short, writing centers, technology, and intellectual property are bound together in a network of narratives (i.e., copyrights, plagiarism, authorship, scholarship, research papers, digital libraries), but the specific aim of this essay is to unencrypt the carceral code of plagiarism. It is important, I think, to *inflect* the foundation narratives that support the fortress in order to make them a little less strange and possibly less dangerous. If, as Haraway reports, there are now patent laws protecting property rights in gene sequences of indigenous peoples, and if we are now banking human diversity to protect difference before it gets engineered out, it may seem ludicrous to be questioning the punitive economy of plagiarism. But this is also what Haraway means by situating writing in an integrated circuitry, and what I mean by situating writing centers in such an economy. In other words, tutoring writing and patenting genomes may have more in common than we imagine.

Plagiarism is situated within a complex matrix in which numerous conceptual sites of struggle compete for our attention. It is especially complex in the field of composition pedagogy where technology now complicates the scene of writing and threatens to expose the very economy that drives the matrix. Technotopia also consists of techno-countercultures (Kroker) that are redefining the conceptual data that hold our teaching together, such master concepts as "text," "author," "literacy," "library," "classroom," "curriculum," and "university." In addition, technology demands that our institutions recognize and "authorize" new modes of intelligibility. Any one of these sites of struggle could map a path to examine plagiarism. My critical coordinates, however, steer us in a more dangerous direction—into an autocritique of the motives that drive our disciplinary policies for plagiarism. I would say that few of us know how to assess new forms of text and authorship, and, thus, few of us know where to draw the line when we suspect a student of plagiarism. We may have successfully killed the romantic myth of authorship and replaced it with the new myth of social construction, but the new myth is still bound to a romantic system of scholarship. We must examine what is at stake in our position as gatekeepers of a outdated system of scholarship that is at odds with the digitotalitarian state in which we now live. It is time to question our complicity in the punitive economy of plagiarism.

To understand our complicity in this relation, let me return to the military analogy a moment. In the history of defense technology, as Manuel DeLanda explains, "the electromagnetic curtains of radar may be seen as a modern-day mutation of the old fortress walls of earth and stone. Understanding the mentality of a citadel under siege ... is essential to understanding what happens to a nation when the old fortress walls are extended through radar to continental proportions" (5). In other words, writing centers, as extensions of classroom pedagogy, are but mutations of the old fortress. And, like composition teachers, tutors fall into the strategic gap between technocentric pedagogy and printcentric peda-gogy. The question to consider is how this gap problematizes the fine line between collaboration and plagiarism.

To use another analogy, let's assume that in the discipline of history some teachers had access to a time machine in which their classes could actually transgress the ideology of printcentrism and enter the time and space of past historical events, while other teachers continued to teach from textbooks, historical biographies, and historical documents. Now, if there were such a thing as a "history center" where all students who studied history came for tutoring, how would such a center construct a philosophy of tutoring? Would they claim that they help students with "any kind of history"? How would we train tutors to migrate from the history experienced through print to the history experienced through technology? Once there, how would such tutoring redraw the param-eters of intellectual real estate? DeLanda claims that in the evolution of war technology it is necessary to understand the transition from weapons to computers by looking back to a time when the logical structures of computer hardware were "once incarnated in the human body in the form of problem-solving recipes" known as heuristics. The migrations oc-curred when such logical structures migrated to the rules that make up logical notations (the syllogism, calculus), and ultimately to electrome-chanical switches and circuits (4). This history is also part of the history of strategic thought and, thus, can be applied to tutoring.

My aim in dramatizing the hypothetical dilemma of history peda-gogy via the history of war technology is to draw a direct comparison to the politics of tutoring in the gap between technocentric pedagogy and printcentric pedagogy. By analyzing the structures that support plagia-rism as a fortress, I propose a radical reconception of the protocols of ownership of both ideas and the expression of ideas, and a reconception of how we use (and perceive) the technoculture that has necessitated this move. In so doing, we must call the priesthood of intellectual property into question, from the copyright legalists and patent-pooling cartels to the universities, the publishers, the teachers, and the tutors. In so doing, we must look for structures that enable the priesthood to function as the gatekeeper in a higher economy of intertextuality rigidly linked to what Stuart Moulthrop calls "information capitalism" (qtd. in Brent 10). The paradox of this economy lies in a certain pathology at work in the infrastructure of the publication of writing, a pathological dis/ease spread among our theories, pedagogies, and publications. A serious contradiction exists between our systems of referential apparatus like citations, which reinforce the fact that knowledge is built communally, and the practice of labelling our creations with the name of its maker, which reinforces the romantic myth of the individual creative genius (roughly paraphrased from a post by some articulate woman on some email list I subscribe to). To further complicate matters, technology highlights this disjunction in exponential ways. Electronic intertextuality launches us into what Arthur Kroker defines as a bimodern age, as "living at the violent edge of primitivism and simulation" (18).

All this to say that we have known, but scarcely theorized, the ways in which representation is problematized by technology. Through certain wormholes in history, from the printing press, to the camera, to digitized images that control smart missiles, the modes of representation and ownership have been irreversibly renegotiated. The questions I pose are partially implicated in this history. For example, I think we must ask ourselves why the fields of art, music, film, photography, graphic design, and architecture, to name a few, have been redefining representation and ownership of creativity for much longer than the field of writing. If writing is the last bastion of primitivism, writing centers, invested as we are in technology, occupy the borderzones of bimodernity. Like amphibians, we live with one foot in primitivism, one foot in simulation. But Kroker reminds us, this is a violent edge. Ask any student who faces the threat of punitive measures for plagiarizing, and ask any tutor who feels the tension of the double bind. I think we cannot be too scrupulous in analyzing the nature of plagiarism and the punitive system that is at stake.

Let me cite a few examples of how deep the punitive current of plagiarism runs, one rather humorous, one not so humorous. Recently, I cruised onto the Infobahn and exited at TexasOwl, an online writing center at the University of Texas at Austin. After navigating my way into the main room of the virtual center, I teleported into a conversation among some of the peer tutors. They were hotly debating whether or not a student someone had tutored had indeed been guilty of plagiarism. I

asked them what they thought should be done, that is, in their role as peer
tutors. One tutor said quickly, "I think we should take the student to the
'Plagiarism Pit O'Hell'"! When I grimaced and asked, "What's that?" he
said, "Oh, that's where we teach students how to cite sources correctly or
be tortured."

At various times, plagiarism has been a hot topic on the MBU
(Megabyte University) e-mail list. Darting around the net like voltage,
some of these thoughts were highly charged with punitive language. It's
"amateur night police work." It's a "dastardly deed." "What motivates
intentional plagiarism, could be laziness, greed, or a desire to trick the
instructor." To which someone responds: "rights of ownership ... are not
as important as the misrepresentation that the student makes to the
instructor." Yes, plagiarism is "an attempt to cheat the system and
perhaps the teacher." The debate took a turn when some suggested that
plagiarism is a teaching problem, not a moral problem. One writing
center director claimed it is a "rhetorical problem" as well, arguing that
"it tends to be a very ineffective strategy for interacting with an audience.
Alienation is a virus, spreading. Plagiarism is a carrier, a plague rat."
Another picked up the cue and voiced concerns about such detective
work, catching the quarry, and being gleeful about it. "Teachers get quite
huffy over student plagiarism, as if students had offended God," they
said, concluding that plagiarism is "a consequence of questionable pedagogy." Someone else replied, "Thanks for reminding us that the enemy
is us." The exchange came to rest here; in fact, the silence following this
admission was deafening as lurkers began to delete the subject headings
RE: PLAGIARISM and SON OF PLAGIARISM. Finally, the messages
stopped coming altogether because tracking our students' "informa-
tional footprints" (Levy 55) led us straight back to the fortress. It seems,
then, that what is at stake in disciplining students for plagiarism has much
more to do with stealing and defying our authority than with creativity.
In other words, the moral crime against established authority bothers us
more than the economic crime that deprives an author of proper compensation for their ideas and the expressions of their ideas. The problem with
plagiarism has to do with breaking a taboo. We all plagiarize. Teachers
are just more clever plagiarists. We are more adept at concealing the
sutures. Yet when students are clumsy plagiarists, or peer tutors inno-
cently aid in this process, they all threaten to expose the whole system.
The priesthood wants to protect the sacred cow; they can't afford to have
it wandering around.

Two questions come to mind for writing centers. To what extent, we
should ask, is the writing center implicated in students' learning to
plagiarize? And to what degree are we also complicit with the punitive
system that brings students in line with a particular morality and a

dominant economy? The answers, I think lie in the classic double bind, the nature of which is found in two aspects of the infrastructure: institutional control of access to knowledge and the system by which access is controlled, testing and grading. In "The Knowledge Machine," Seymour Papert explains that educational institutions are in the business of "mediated acquisition" of knowledge (52). That is, having created a system of knowledge by subject and by grade (e.g., 4th, 5th, junior, senior), and achievement by test scores, institutions deny access to knowledge by breaking up knowledge into pre-digested units. Once students had technological access to knowledge, Papert claims, the "possibility of freely exploring [and creating] worlds of knowledge calls into question the very idea of an administered curriculum" (50). Dale Spender agrees, noting that "academic knowledge stands to lose its status and privileged position because electronic knowledge is difficult to verify" and to enter into our current system of accountability, academic scholarship (31). The question to consider now is how we got ourselves into this mess.

According to John Perry Barlow, co-founder of the Electronic Frontier Foundation, "digital technology is detaching information from the physical plane, where property law of all sorts has always found definition" (85). In other words, copyright law was invented to protect expression and, Barlow notes, "with few exceptions ..., to express was to make physical" (85). And to make public. Thus, the priesthood of publication has established a system of accountability and compensation based upon physical and public products. But, Barlow asks, how can we "protect new forms of property with old methods" (85)? "What are the essential characteristics of unbounded creation? How does it differ from previous forms of property?" (89). It is my view that this product mentality, fueled by its reliance on that which is physical and public, feeds the impulse to grade and constrains the evolution of new forms of writing and the institutional recognition of new modes of intelligibility. If, as Barlow suggests, "digitized information has no 'final cut,'" don't we really just "franchise" the "precise turn of phrase used to convey a particular idea" (90, 85)? Jacques Derrida asks a similar question: if educational institutions are more interested in the publication of knowledge, rather than knowledge itself, "where is the beginning of publication?" (19). How do we compensate (and copyright) genres of writing that do not conform to the old methods of protection of property? Barlow lists jazz improvisations, stand-up comedy routines, mime performances, developing monologues, and unrecorded broadcast transmissions as expressions that "lack [the] Constitutional requirement of fixation as a 'writing'" (90). According to Barlow's two predictions, we will come to value "real-time performance" over "discrete bundles of that which is being shown" (128), and to value service, where you serve the industry by enhancing your product or someone's product rather than packaging it and selling it.

In a sense, Barlow suggests, "the future protection of your intellectual property will depend on your ability to control your relationship to the market [and] the value of that relationship will reside in the quality of performance, the validity of your expertise, its relevance to your market, and, underlying everything, the ability of that market to access your creative services swiftly, conveniently, and interactively" (128). Spender calls the new system, "perform or perish" (28). In other words, she writes, "publishers, in selecting titles, now want to know whether the author is promotable and can perform the work" (37). Even some of our most medieval writing rituals, like the dissertation, will be on video or conducted online at a MOO with scholars and committee members discussing the research with the doctoral candidate (see Lingua MOO transcript). The upshot of all of this can be interpreted positively. Barlow predicts that "the failure of law [or, in our case, grades, or traditional dissertation defenses] will almost certainly result in a compensating re-emergence of ethics as the ordering template of society" (128).

Still, it becomes more and more difficult to sort through the legalities of intellectual property law as the rapid movement toward free access to information (as well as recombinations of information) becomes embroiled in the simultaneous bureaucratic movement against electronic privacy. As this conflict plays itself out on the commercial and political scene, writing centers can learn from recent developments in art, music, and electronic subcultures that have redefined notions of authorship and ownership. For example, many writers, artists, and musicians who experiment with what some call "positive plagiarism," or "sampling," are often accused of "theft of information" or "piracy." Yet sampling, which brings in the unexpected or "inappropriate" to construct a retro/garde of "appropriating" other creative work (old and new), is considered a valid way of "doing" art among many artists and writers. Bob Cook works, for example, to call attention to the possibilities of manipulating an original. He perceives his digitized/colorized images of Ansel Adams' photographs as a translation of an original or a visual quotation. Ardele Lister, film and video artist at Rutgers, explains her approach: "I use archival bits from many different films, editing them together to make the meaning I want .... I work in the forms of my time—media—I address those forms and I cannibalize them, as images and structures" (81-82). Artists, like Lister and Cook, use the Retro principle, "a constant shifting of language and perspective for comparative analysis. Unlike postmodernism, which decontextualizes found elements to produce faux novelty, [Retro] recontextualizes identifiable motifs 'sampled' from art and music history, creating faux canons" (Laddish 68). One record label called Re-Constriction

Records actually promotes itself as "the New Breed of Techno-Thug-gery." A graphic design company, Designers Republic, whose visual language of advertising has been dubbed "American Expressionism," is "noted for their computerish lettertypes and use of corporate logos, both hijacked and parodied, the Republic's mutated multinational hiero-glyphics form a global slang for an unashamedly sample-based rave generation—Westinghouse meets Smiley culture" (Marshall 100). As Ian Anderson, its founder, says of corporate logos, "'Sure we rip them off, but we use them out of context to say something new .... People today like the idea of being their own corporations rather than being taken over by one'" (100). Working against the "fictional artists," Stewart Home called for a "refusal of creativity" from 1990-93 during which artists would refuse to make, sell, or exhibit art to force the market to collapse in order for artists to be able to take control of the means by which their work was distrib-uted. Home's notion of "positive plagiarism" and his habit of assuming multiple names challenged the identity politics linked to the ideas of property and ownership. It was Home who proposed that all magazines change their name to *SMILE.* In the winter of 1988, Home organized the "Festival of Plagiarism" in London, which included an unjuried group show in which all work was attributed to Karen Elliot, one of Home's multiple names. The festival "served as both a critique of serious culture ... and as a platform for alternatives to the elitism of ruling-class art" (Home 32).

It seems, then, that who gets in/corporated in the current retribalization is as much an issue of ethics and access as it is self-mutation. More and more students will become what Brenda Laurel calls "fusion people" students who have combined majors in, say, ethno-graphic studies and computer science (Morgan 84). Our tutoring and teaching practices have to adapt to these new fusions, genres, media, and cultural practices, or we will find ourselves on the wrong side of the fortress when it gets overrun. As Richard Lanham suggests, print is a "philosophic medium," the "electronic screen a deeply 'rhetorical' one" (xii). In some ways, then, our current quarrel is really a very old one. We stand at the point of an ancient tension between philosophy and rhetoric, but with the addition of at least two new tropes into the dialectic—speed and virtuality. If, as Paul Virilio argues, "the fortified town is an immobile machine, the military engineer's specific task is to fight against its inertia. 'The goal of fortification is not to stop armies, to contain them, but to dominate, even to facilitate their movements'" (12). If we are to shed our military engineer personae, to resist the temptation to contain, dominate, and control our students' textual movements, we must face several realities. The speed of digital movement forces us to face the rapid growth of free access to information and the implications of this freedom on the "administered curriculum" of higher education and the punitive guards that protect the fortress. Virtuality forces us to redefine our perceptions of collaboration, surveillance, and identity in terms of multivalence, confluence, and hypertext authorship. It forces us to question the problem of ownership and authorship if a hypertext user can "create a whole basket of links and 'publish' this as a kind of sampler, anthology, or work of criticism" ("Hypertext" 146). It forces us to acknowledge that a punitive economy of plagiarism merely fortifies the market and encourages a stealth pedagogy. It is time to teach and tutor writing in a new context, in a situated electronic context in which technology is redefining subjectivity and spatiality and in which the law is struggling "to define its application in a context where fundamental notions of speech, property and place take profoundly new forms" (Electronic 88). What is needed is a retro-tool for "provoking a little technical and political intercourse, or criminal conversation, or reproductive commerce" (Haraway, "Modest") about what counts as writing, what counts as pedagogy, and what counts as property.

Works Cited

Barlow, John Perry. "The Economy of Ideas: A Framework for Patents and Copyrights in the Digital Age." *WIRED* 2.3 (1994): 84-90, 126-29.

Branwyn. Gareth. "Street Noise." *MONDO 2000* 7 (1992): 30.

Brent, Doug. "Oral Knowledge, Typographic Knowledge, Electronic Knowledge: Speculations on the History of Ownership." *Intertek* 3.4 (1993): 4-11.

Cook, Bob. Personal interview, Feb. 1994. University of Texas at Arlington.

De Landa, Manuel. *War in the Age of Intelligent Machines*. New York: Zone, 1991.

Derrida, Jacques. "Mochlos; or, The Conflict of the Faculties." *Logomachia: The Conflict of the Faculties*. Ed. Richard Rand. Lincoln: U of Nebraska P, 1992. 1-34.

Electronic Frontier Foundation. *MONDO 2000 User's Guide to the New Edge*. New York: Harper Perennial. 88-89.

Haraway, Donna. "Modest Witness @ Second Millennium. The Female Man © Meets OncoMouse™." Unpublished paper delivered at Southern Methodist University, April, 1994.

—. *Simians, Cyborgs, and Women: The Reinvention of Nature*. New York: Routledge, 1991.

Home, Stewart. "To Tell the Truth." *lightworks* 19 (1988/89): 30-32.

"Hypertext." *MONDO 2000 User's Guide to the New Edge*. New York: Harper Perennial. 146-49.

Kroker, Arthur. *The Possessed Individual: Technology and the French Postmodern*. New York: St. Martin's, 1992.

Laddish, Kenneth. "The Fab Vier: Dissecting the Body Politic." *Mondo 2000* 9 (1993): 66-77.

Lanham, Richard A. *The Electronic Word: Democracy, Technology, and the Arts*. Chicago: U of Chicago P, 1993.

Levy, Steven. "Crypto Rebels." *WIRED* 1.2 (1993): 54-61.

Lingua MOO Archive. Transcript of Dene Grigar's Doctoral Defense, held at University of Texas at Dallas, July 25, 1995 online at Lingua MOO (Archive link at URL: http://mohawk.utdallas.edu:7000).

Lister, Ardele. "A Brief Conversation Between Ardele Lister and Pat McCoy." *FELIX* 1.3 (1993): 80-82.

Marshall, Jules. "Designers Republic: Visual Sampling for the Digital Generation." *WIRED* 2.4 (1994): 100.

Morgan, Jas. "Brenda Laurel the Lizard Queen: Interview." *MONDO 2000* 7 (1992): 82-89.

Papert, Seymour. "Obsolete Skill Set: The 3Rs." *WIRED* 1.2 (1993): 50-52.

Spender, Dale. "Electronic Scholarship: Perform or Perish?" *Women, Information Technology, Scholarship.* Ed. H. Jeanie Taylor, Cheris Kramaral, and Maureen Ebben. Urbana: U of Illinois P, 1993. 28-43.

Virilio, Paul. *Speed and Politics: An Essay on Dromology.* Trans. Mark Polizzotti. New York: Semiotexte, 1986.

"Industrial Strength Tutoring": Strategies for Handling "Customer Complaints"

Cheryl Reed
San Diego Mesa College

While I was a graduate teaching assistant, I participated in a committee project to improve relations among teaching assistants, students, and faculty in the Writing Program for which I worked. The most profitable area of my research for the committee took me to a section of the downtown public library intriguingly headed "industrial psychology." Wavering between visions of distressed factory equipment lying on the analyst's couch, or bald-headed genies powerfully cleaning—one's psyche—I leafed through the predictable, top-down management theory that tells administrators how to get more out of their perennially inefficient staffs. But on another shelf, toward the back, in the dark, lurked a sub-genre. It sported books with cheery, self-help titles that I was embarrassed to carry through the check-out line, titles like *How to Work for a Jerk* or *If You Want Guarantees, Buy a Toaster.* These books were flippant, irreverent, and unequivocally practical—some of them bitingly so. They said things like "A difficult boss can be a personal disaster .... you're unlikely to be rescued by anyone else in your organization" (Bramson 5) and "as long as you believe that all actions in the office are based on fairness and rationality, you'll be hurt, confused, and disillusioned" (Kennedy 12). My personal favorite was the one that thanked its author's first boss "for making me aware that serious mental disturbance and success are not mutually exclusive" (Bing acknowledgments.)

What these books offered in common was the potential of "leverage" (what we might call "agency") through a recognition and manipulation of the structures operating within an institutionally empowered, alien discourse—that of the boss, the supervisor, the corporation. In this respect, I found industrial psychology to be remarkably similar to student-centered pedagogy. Both sets of theories address the process of constructing a subjectivity that is legible and that carries weight within the discursive system in which one functions. However we configure the student/instructor relationship—as mentorship, as collaboration, as empowerment—it is an integral part of a hierarchical network of task-oriented agents carrying on the "enterprise" of the university.

In saying this, I am attempting to reinvent a much-despised metaphor—one that operates simultaneously with the "family" metaphors Dawn Formo critiques (see Formo and Welsh in this volume) and that is at least as often, and as vehemently, denied. I am speaking of education as a business, with knowledge (or astute workers) as its product. While teaching and tutoring are certainly not the mere transmission of skills—the exchange of "goods and services"—they often get configured as such when the values of collaboration, empowerment, and re-visioning run aground on the rocks of evaluation. When students complain about grades, as often happens, and writing gets posed as a "company product" or grades as a form of "paycheck," the students themselves are invoking business models. The tutoring session thus becomes a contest of metaphors.

In practice, however, these seemingly incongruous discourses always already exist side by side in the writing center. To mix metaphors a bit, we might term the writing center a *family business*, one that provides (however inconsistently or imperfectly) its practitioners emotional, economic, and "belongingness" needs at the same time it offers a service its "clients" need and want. Its "production" and administrative functions often overlap intense interpersonal ties and emotional investments. Tutors who aren't trained to negotiate this strange mix are at a decided disadvantage.

Let's look for a moment at the inherently conflicted institutional position of the writing instructor/tutor—academia's version of "middle management."

In larger universities or multidisciplinary centers, instructors and tutors—who are often students, themselves—are not necessarily versed in composition theory and may not teach their chosen disciplines; they do not choose reading assignments or paper topics; they cannot change assignment loads or due dates; and they cannot redirect student projects into promising tangential excursions. Many times instructors work under a different "boss" each quarter, or have multiple bosses whose mandates conflict with each other and/or the instructor's own academic aims, needs, or disciplinary training. The instructor's paycheck may be regarded institutionally as "financial aid" and is generally inadequate. Further, students often resent or distrust an instructor's own student status and question the legitimacy of his or her authority to evaluate writing. Finally, the evaluations regarding all of these considerations become part of the file that determines an instructor's future ability to obtain a "real" job. Writing instructors and tutors are rarely adequately or specifically trained to negotiate their vulnerable and heavily politicized positions. But they should be.

For our writing program, I suggested various ways—from more direct apprenticing of graduate instructors to constructing wider-based performance evaluations—that writing program graduate staff might be formed into a network of highly qualified almost-professionals motivated to do the very job the program required. In this article, I want to focus on a tiny part of that—solutions offered by industrial psychology for the inevitable "family squabbles" that occur within the professor/instructor-tutor/student triad. These potentially volatile interactions, which tend to surface in the relative intimacy of the tutoring session, not only express concern about our "product"—education—but bring up questions of "family" loyalty. Often, student angst expresses ambivalence and insecurity about the instructor-tutor's position and function in the "corporation" and in the "family."

In offering the following scenarios, my goal is not, of course, to maneuver the student out of expressing his or her complaint. Rather, I hope to direct the tutoring session away from emotion-laden dead ends into a problem-solving mode that promotes fruitful revision and action. Understanding the power dynamics inherent in business relationships can help tutors get things back on track.

Scenario I: Writing Program

A teaching assistant who leads discussion sections for a large lecture class has just returned graded papers. Although the lecturer assigns course readings and paper topics, (s)he has no interest in seeing the resulting exams and papers. The teaching assistant both coaches students in negotiating assigned topics and evaluates them on their performances. Because the instructor both does and does not carry authority to fashion class parameters, his/her tutoring function is often viewed by students as an imposition of low-priority goals and standards arbitrarily conceived outside of "real" course content.

TUTOR: Hello, Tracy. Have some questions about your paper?

STUDENT: Well, yeah. Why did you give me a C? My roommate got an A, and (s)he didn't even start writing until the night before it was due!

A variation of this opening runs as follows:

STUDENT: I've *never* gotten *any* grade less than an A. All of my *other* instructors have given me A's, my high school teachers gave me A's, my mother thinks I should get A's, and she's been a teacher for thirty-two years.

Both of these openings assume a "middle-management" function for the instructor/tutor. They focus on the institutional position of the tutor—a position frankly interchangeable with others of like rank, perhaps unevenly performed, and certainly fair game for comparison with those (by far superior) workers outside the institution. Confronted with this not-so-implicit questioning of his/her ability to function within a hard-won and emotionally demanding position in the "family business," the instructor/tutor's initial response might be to defend his or her expertise by showing the student just how wrong-headed her paper really is. The student, however, is most likely viewing herself as a salesperson "pitching" her ideas to a mid-level employee—who is management with no real decision-making power in the institution at large, but who unfortunately has been given jurisdiction over her work. Pointing out her work's flaws will force her into an even more fervent "sales pitch." What the student probably needs is some sort of reassurance that the university system (the tutor's "product") will work for the student as well—that the grade isn't personal and the tutor thinks she can, indeed, live up to university standards. The instructor/tutor can profitably reinvent the scenario by positioning the student as *client* rather than peer evaluator.

TUTOR: Well, I can't really change your *roommate's* grade on the basis of *your* paper, but I can take your work home and take another look at it. Why don't you tell me in your own words the writing strategies you feel my comments address. What should I focus on?

Since the student is obviously emotional at this point of the interchange, and since the instructor may be veering that way in response to her, the instructor reacts as customer ("Clarify your proposition and I'll think it over"—the salesperson's nightmare) and then subtly shifts his or her own role to that of salesperson. While (s)he refuses to negotiate his or her position in the academy by utilizing the paper grade as evidence, (s)he directly addresses this manifestly tangential issue by invoking equally tangential "company policy" ("I can't change your roommate's grade—"), and offering "customer service" ("What I can do, however, is take another look"). This action puts some distance and cooling off time between tutor and irate student, while offering a serious look into the student's "customer complaint" ("What should I focus on?").

While the instructor/tutor's goal here is, of course, to refocus the interchange toward the student's writing (the "real" issue in the tutoring session), his or her tacit reassertion of the tutor's role as institutionally-authorized collaborator may bring on a corresponding shift in the student's resistance to that role. As the instructor/tutor aligns him or herself with institutional policies and goals, phase two of the interchange may resemble the following:

STUDENT: The most important focus is obviously *my grade!* You won't allow me to revise this paper for a re-grade, so what good does reading your comments do? All I want is an A out of this course to keep my scholarship, please my parents, and ...

The student/client, no longer overtly questioning the tutor's job performance, reassigns the tutor the role of "company rep," the manipulator of the bureaucratic maze, the powerful gatekeeper who stands between the student and doom. (Note: This type of no-revision dead end usually occurs in "core" sequences that attempt to cover a great deal of course material while at the same time imposing heavy writing requirements.) One response might be—

TUTOR: Of course you're concerned with your grade because you're a responsible student who cares about her work. You're obviously not a "C" student—it's just that *this paper* has some problem areas.

The tutor again avoids meta-issues such as his or her own responsibility to justify top-down "corporate" policies that allow no revisions and no "play" in minimum scholarship requirements. Instead, (s)he reaffirms the student's value as a "client" or "fellow worker" ("You're a responsible student who cares—") and refocuses the student's attention on their common problem (a "C" paper) rather than on the student's "product management deficiency" or "job performance" (not a "C" student). Despite personally disappointing results, the tutor implies, the student plays an integral part in the family business.

Another tutor response might be—

TUTOR: You're right; we're not set up to revise papers in Lit 1-2-3; there's just too much material to cover. But I wanted to find ways to help all of you package things more clearly the next time around—because, of course, the university usually measures how much you know by the words you put on paper. Now! Let's talk about these comments in the margin, here.

With this type of response, the tutor, having constructed an institutional position as "sales rep" or "experienced employee," acknowledges the inherent limitations of his or her "corporation's" hierarchical, bureaucratic structure and agrees that the student has pinpointed a problem in "product management." Importantly, (s)he follows this winsome honesty with an offer to help the student around the pitfalls ahead through a better understanding of the corporate system ("the university usually measures how much you know—") and product ("let's look at—").

Each of these responses directs the student back to her own writing processes and offers strategies in negotiating a frustrating, contradictory set of requirements and demands. Meta-discussions regarding tutor competence or institutional structure are tabled to focus on the student's immediate needs. Next, let's look at a scenario in which student concern over "corporate policy" is, indeed, the central focus.

Scenario II: Writing Center

A tutor has coached a student through a paper assignment for Professor Smith. The professor (who thinks the writing center staff exists to "help people clear up spelling and grammar snafus") has total control over the assignment's topic, conventions, format, and presentation. It is this professor's responsibility to assign grades.

TUTOR: Hello, Steve. How are you doing?

STUDENT: Well, not too good. Professor Smith gave me an F on that paper you helped me with. I've got it right here somewhere (searches in backpack).

At this point, the tutor, who has no control over "product" or "personnel" evaluation, can't be sure why this student has scheduled an appointment. Does he want encouragement? revenge? help with revisions? How is he constructing the tutor's "corporate" role? Has he come to the wrong "department" with his "customer complaint"?

STUDENT: Here it is. I'm really upset. Look at what he wrote on page 3—"This is the worst paper I've ever read in my twenty years of teaching experience." And look here on page 5—"How could you even think of arguing something so ridiculous?" And then he took off ten points because I skipped lines between paragraphs instead of indenting them! And I don't even think he read past this page ...

At this point, it's clear that "company policy" or "performance evaluation standards" must be addressed before "project development" can continue. Even if the professor's comments are valid critiques of this student's writing, phrasing them as attacks on his intelligence has undermined his ability to think about possible revisions. Before (s)he can encourage the student, however, the tutor may have to deal with personal anger that an "executive" would insult a "client" or "inexperienced employee" this way, misrepresenting corporate goals and offering no clue what steps might be taken to improve "product" or "performance."

At the same time, the tutor's response may be limited by his or her "middle management" position in the institution, and/or by "company policies" that require unequivocal support of the "higher ups." In any case, the tutor can respond with an acknowledgment of the student's effort and his current feelings of distress.

TUTOR: I know this must be a big blow to you, because I watched you work hard on that paper ...

STUDENT (interrupting): I mean, Professor Smith is such a jerk. Everybody thinks so. The other day he asked if we had any questions about his lecture, and when my friend asked him something, he said, "If you'd been listening, you'd know the answer to that question."

Clearly, this "executive's" behavior is out of line. The student needs to know that this treatment of him was, to say the least, unfortunate. The tutor can, without denigrating the professor's personality or pedagogy, express his or her concern for this student as a responsive representative of the "company."

TUTOR: I'm so sorry you got hurt by this.

Although (s)he has not assigned blame, the tutor as "company rep" or "middle management" has acknowledged that acts performed in the name of the "company," even those undertaken by a "corporate executive," can misfire or have adverse effects. The tutor's next move will be dictated by "company policies" regarding corporate missteps as well as by the institutional support network that undergirds "middle-management" employees. Whatever specific grievance policies allow, however, the tutor now directs his or her energies to problem-solving strategies. What options are open to this client/inexperienced employee?

TUTOR: So, what do you think you're going to do about this? How much does this affect your GPA? Can you revise? Do you want to talk to Professor Smith, maybe get him to explain what he didn't like about your paper?

Having acknowledged that the student's self-esteem was justifiably bruised, the tutor directs him toward active responses that could lead to a resolution of his writing problems. In the real-time instance upon which this scenario was based, the tutor spent the remainder of the session discussing strategies by which the student could approach the offending (and offensive) professor with a neutral, business-like stance aimed at what we might call "project development." This particular tutor, happily employed in a program that had some say in professorial treatment of students, also informed writing center administrators of the professor's inappropriate remarks so that they could be addressed by those with higher "management" positions. Whatever institutional restrictions the tutor must operate within, however, his or her "client" remains the primary concern.

Conclusion

Student-centered pedagogy assumes the tutor to be a vital institutional link for students alienated by the confusing and contradictory demands they must negotiate at the university. Perhaps because of this role as liaison, tutors find they must enact a powerful mix of rather intimate relational bonds. Often, tutors find themselves performing conflicted roles with mediated authority; occupying both student and instructor positions in the university's "family business," they stand as academia's version of "middle management." Thus, industrial psychology's examination of effective political and relational strategies within business organizations aligns with student-centered pedagogy's recognition of the very intimate nature of the student/professor/tutor triad. A theoretical "merger" can enable the writing center to construct— if not the illusory community of scholars we so love to envision—at least a temporary alliance of colleagues whose individual areas of expertise promote the functional administration of the "family business."

Works Cited

Bing, Stanley. *Crazy Bosses: Spotting Them, Serving Them, Surviving Them.* New York: Morrow , 1992.

Bramson, Robert. *Coping with Difficult Bosses.* New York: Carol, 1992.

Kennedy, Marilyn Moats. *Office Politics: Seizing Power, Wielding Clout.* Chicago: Follett, 1980.

For Further Reading

Bell, Robert. *You Can Win at Office Politics: Techniques, Tips, and Step-by-Step Plans for Coming Out Ahead.* New York: Times, 1984.

Bell applies games theory to office politics to suggest ways to continue a successful career despite hierarchical power plays within the institution for which one works.

Benton, D. A. *Lions Don't Need to Roar: Using the Leadership Power of Professional Presence to Stand Out, Fit In, and Move Ahead.* New York: Warner, 1992.

This text focuses on strategies for constructing a professional subjectivity in the business hierarchy.

Elgin, Suzette Haden. *The Last Word on the Gentle Art of Verbal Self-Defense.* New York: Prentice, 1987.

—. *More on the Gentle Art of Verbal Self-Defense.* New York: Prentice, 1986.

While these texts are not industrial psychology *per se,* they both focus on linguistic/rhetorical analysis of emotionally charged verbal exchanges to suggest responses that minimize, undercut, or redirect the rhetorical structures occupied by both participants. The aim of this maneuvering is to prevent assumed/implied meanings from engendering powerful emotions and thus getting the exchange of information off track.

Grothe, Mardy, and Peter Wylie. *Problem Bosses: Who They Are and How to Deal with Them.* New York: Facts on File , 1987.

Examines common communications problems within bureaucracies to suggest alternatives that empower middle management.

Hochheiser, Robert M. *How to Work for a Jerk: Your Success is the Best Revenge.* New York: Vintage, 1987.

Hochheiser's dedication says it all: "To the bosses of the world, without whom I wouldn't have been exposed to the pettiness and stupidity that inspired this book." Wittily angry, the text suggests strategies to avoid unintentional victimization in a highly-politicized environment.

—. *If You Want Guarantees, Buy a Toaster.* New York: Morrow, 1991.

This text focuses particularly on survival strategies for the employee made vulnerable through corporate shakeups such as mergers, downsizings, and revolving-door executives.

Jaffe, Betsy. *Altered Ambitions: What's Next in Your Life?* New York: Fine, 1991.

Targeting the female worker for whom job-market opportunities and role expectations have shifted radically during the past few decades, Jaffe sets up a coping style continuum and suggests how apparently contradictory strategies can be combined to enhance one's personal and positional negotiations of stress.

Kennedy, Marilyn Moats. *Office Warfare: Strategies For Getting Ahead In The Aggressive 80's.* New York: Macmillan, 1985.

A bit bloody, this text focuses on the institution in political crisis. Looks at/suggests maneuverings within hierarchical business relationships when the overall structure is shaky or is being dismantled.

Solomon, Muriel. *Getting Praised, Raised, and Recognized.* New Jersey: Prentice, 1993.

Efficiently organized into pithy bits of advice regarding institutional politics, this text is unfortunately based on management's perspective; that is, it shows the employee how to operate within a disempowered position rather then empowering him/her within whatever position he/she occupies. This advice needs to be detoxed from the constant reiteration of the employee's having his or her personal being defined by employer.

Tickling the Student's Ear: Collaboration and the Teacher/Student Relationship

Dawn M. Formo
Jennifer Welsh

University of Southern California

For the Greeks, education meant, essentially, a profound and intimate relationship, a personal union between a young man and an elder who was at once his model, his guide and his initiator—a relationship onto which the fire of passion threw warm and turbid reflections. (Marrou 31)

•A frustrated student stops the writing instructor after class to explain that his peer revision isn't working. He whines, "They don't tell me what I need to know to get a good grade from you."

In another scene,

•An assignment asking for personal reflection on a life-changing event produces two papers recounting sexual abuse and rape. The instructor must decide whether and how to intervene.

and finally,

•A male first-year composition instructor works to establish a personal connection with his students to counteract the authoritarian institution while a female first-year composition instructor works to establish authority to be taken seriously by her students.

These incidents are real. And their respective realities reveal that teacher/student relationships have a history of being simultaneously intimate and hierarchical while also being influenced by gender. Our field of composition theory has shifted away from product-oriented approaches that concentrate on correct punctuation and grammar toward student-centered pedagogies that emphasize the writer's process. Because of this shift, the theory of composition pedagogy has become inescapably entwined with the dynamics of the teacher/student relationship.

A central component of this trend, collaboration theory, rests on the notion that the hierarchical relationship between teacher and student obscures the less powerful voice and inhibits any dialogue in the classroom. While the benefits of collaborative practices are commonly noted,[1] the complex interpersonal dynamics these practices carry with them need to be explored further.

The power and closeness inherent in this relationship are complicated by the historical influences that define our perceptions of the activity of writing. The structure of English departments and our common notions of the writer have roots in a particular version of the Romantic tradition.[2]

Current collaborative theory is a resistance to a Romantic ideology that privileges the inner voice over the writer's social context. The Romantic figure of the genius-writer out on the moor describes only those who had the socio-economic privilege to withdraw from the public and domestic spheres of production. The other significant hallmark of this Romantic writer is that the decision of what counted as a natural, individual voice was dictated by certain members of an elite group.

This Romantic concept of writing is not simply historical; students bring into our classrooms the belief that, even though they are part of a workshop composition class of 22 writers, they will write their papers by waiting for the inspiration of some natural voice while isolated in their dorm rooms. That they come to writing classes with this attitude is what makes the introduction of collaborative approaches to learning and writing especially challenging for teachers.

Collaborative practices simultaneously attempt to work against this notion of the isolated writer and to provide a more egalitarian classroom environment by encouraging dialogue among peers and between teacher and student. Some teachers interested in collaboration attempt to shift power from themselves to the students by implementing expressivist pedagogy, which privileges the "natural voice" of the student. One recent textbook advocating this approach through journal writing explains, "When you write a journal you are writing only for yourself, and if you do it enough, sooner or later you will learn to recognize your natural voice" (Winkler and McCuen 3). While this approach seemingly hands over authority to the voice of the individual student, it quickly becomes clear that it is the teacher who has the power to decide which of the student's expressions represent her "true voice," and ultimately to evaluate that voice, thus returning the classroom to a hierarchal structure.

In addition, while collaborative practices that draw on expressivist theories aim to provide everyone the opportunity to speak, they do not necessarily promote a dialogue between these voices. In fact, in the title of William E. Coles' book, *The Plural I—and After,* the only plurality is in the voices within a writer's head that are synthesized into a unified position; in other words, expressivism is simply a dialogue within the Romantic self.[3] In the class that is the subject of his text, Coles insists, "Whatever answers you reach in this course, they will be your own. You will do your own learning" (13).

Recent pedagogical theories that aim to break down the hierarchy and separation between teacher and student often only reinscribe it. These contradictions also create difficulties in the interpersonal relationships between teachers and students.

Both collaboration and expressionism share the idea of close, personal interaction between teacher and student as well as between students. Because writing pedagogy, if not all pedagogy, is rooted in classical rhetorical education, the Greek mentor/student model may be the origin of this emphasis on close, personal relationships in education.[4] Inherent in this model is an erotic relationship between teacher and student. The eroticism represented in Plato's *Phaedrus,* for instance, is based on an inequality of knowledge and power but also on a mutual interdependence that creates anxiety for the teacher. In the Greek model of rhetorical education, the bond of intimacy between the scholar and his pupil ensured the transmission of truth rather than simply sophistry. While the student was dependent on the teacher and perhaps exploited by him, the teacher was also dependent on the student for sexual companionship and a justification for the teacher's higher position. Western higher education still draws on this model of rhetorical pedagogy, and the main principles of composition theory are grounded in this tradition, but, in importing the structure and principles of this model, we must also deal with the associations of power and eroticism that accompany them.

Historically, writing has been taught in more intimate environments than other subjects. The fact that composition classes on most campuses are considerably smaller than the first- and second-year courses in other departments illustrates this perceived intimate nature of writing instruction. Implementing collaborative pedagogy within the power dynamics of current classrooms is a struggle against a variety of forces. But the real complexity of collaborative theory lies in the roles it asks teachers and students to play.

Collaboration has most often been discussed in composition circles in terms of colleague-to-colleague interactions. The most cited text in collaboration theory, *Women's Ways of Knowing: The Development of Self, Voice, and Mind* by Belenky, Clinchy, Goldberger, and Tarule, is, in fact, less often cited for its observations about collaboration than it is for the fact that the authors collaborated in writing it. Discussing collaboration in the context of the unequal power dynamics of the teacher/student relationship is a much more complex endeavor, one that Paul Heilker confronts in his article, "Nothing Personal: Twenty-Five Forays Into the Personal in (My) Composition Pedagogy." Heilker insists that, regardless of our intentions, we enter into personal relationships with our students that can have both parental and sexual connotations. This pedagogical reality becomes even more pronounced in collaborative classrooms that aim to level power structures and allow room for all voices to speak.

The one-on-one conference between teacher and student is one of the most common tools used in collaborative teaching. While this type of collaboration has the potential to be a truly equal partnership in working on a paper, it is also the point at which both parties must negotiate the precarious boundary between the two levels of power established by the academic institution. A common scenario might be the following: The teacher challenges the student's language in a paper by suggesting that, in fact, there may be a more effective way for the student to articulate his thought and then offers an example in the language of the academic discourse community. The student recognizes that this is the language he needs to enter the academy, and he quickly comments, "I wish that I had a tape recorder" or asks the teacher to repeat the phrase. Not wanting her own words to be used, the teacher seemingly retracts the statement by telling the student to use his own words. It is the point at which the teacher says, "Use your own words," that the power boundaries become most evident. The teacher is invested in two goals simultaneously. As an educator, she is invested in helping the student make the transition into the academy by acquiring the passwords, but, as a member of that academy, she is invested in maintaining its status above the student apprentice. She therefore refuses to allow the student to use her actual words. Her action suggests that the student must enter the academy by using his own language, language the student has already been told is inadequate.[5]

The tension between these academic positions makes the linguistic boundaries of the academy apparent. The language the academy uses to describe itself often draws on the metaphor of the family, which suggests the following associations: a desire to distinguish itself from outsiders, to acknowledge the hierarchical and competitive relationships among individuals, and to reinforce the protective nature of the teacher/student relationship. In fact, here at USC, the administration commonly refers to the community as the Trojan Family. Within this family metaphor, collaboration becomes a threat to taboos of intimacy. Any relationship between teacher and student threatens the different levels of power within the academic family and is therefore a form of incest. This incest can take two forms. The first is the relationship between members of the same status (e.g., cousin to cousin or student to student). The risk of such a relationship is that it can produce an unhealthy similarity, one of which students are aware. For example, the students who are asked to collaborate with other students often comment that what they really want is the teacher's feedback, as if working with another student is multiplying ignorance rather than gaining access to the higher status language.[6] Similarly, relationships between cousins or siblings are prohibited because the blood lines are too similar. But the benefit of this type of "incestuous" relationship is what Bakhtin terms heteroglossia. While students may not realize it, the strength of the peer's voice lies in its difference, not in its superiority. If they do not recognize that, despite their shared status, their experiences generate multiple voices, they will be unable to value the peer exchange. But, before students can recognize the value of sharing knowledge horizontally as well as vertically, the institution must value and model it.

In its second form, incest in the academy is between members at different levels (e.g., parent to child or teacher to student). The danger of this form, from the perspective of those in power, is that it threatens the academy's status, identity, and purpose by potentially dissolving the distinction between the positions. The danger for the student is that she may lose her right to her own language. On the other hand, this form can provide students with the benefit of a strong model both linguistically and professionally and can develop true heteroglossia within the university that values both students' and teachers' voices.

Because of this tension between encouraging intimacy and maintaining distinct boundaries, metaphors of the writing instructor-student relationship have evolved that sanction this intimacy but establish taboos that protect the individuality and status of the respective members to varying degrees.

Perhaps the most common metaphor used in describing writing instructors is that of the mother (one which is not surprising considering that 65% to 70% of composition instructors are women). This metaphor allows for close and protective personal involvement that nurtures the student through his or her induction into the academy. At the same time, the familial nature of the metaphor establishes an incest taboo that works to prevent this bond from becoming too close.[7]

In *Textual Carnivals: The Politics of Composition*, Susan Miller refers to the composition instructor's role as maid, one which is particularly relevant to graduate students who teach composition. Composition studies has only recently been seen as a scholarly discipline in and of itself; most universities view it as a service to other "more" legitimate disciplines. Universities employ graduate students to teach these courses often at exploitive wages as a means of preparing undergraduates for their "real courses." In this service position, the composition instructor works as a conduit for the student to pass from apprentice status to privileged status within the discourse community. Yet the graduate student who plays this role is simultaneously in the family and in service to the family. Thus, the relationship requires a closeness that threatens institutional, physical, and psychological boundaries. Yet the taboos prohibiting intimacy are not as strong because the graduate student does not share the authority of the mother figure.

The doctor/patient metaphor has been the most common metaphor of writing pedagogy.[8] You may have heard writing centers referred to as writing clinics and writing labs. In terms of medical language, the midwife metaphor is especially common because of the preponderance of women in the field, the collaborative nature of this image, and the way writers talk about writing as childbirth.[9] With this metaphor, the physical boundaries between teacher and student are most threatened. In the midwife metaphor, the writing teacher takes on a much more active role in the "birthing" of the writer's text, to the point that her effort and control over the process are commingled with the student's. Because of her role as midwife, she potentially transgresses both the physical and psychological boundaries dividing herself and the student.[10]

Because these metaphors are ways of thinking and acting[11] that do not necessarily imply codified institutional constraints, the limits that they place on the collaborative teacher/student relationship are tentative at best. This ambiguity leads to two current debates within the academy, those of intellectual property[12] and sexual harassment.[13] While we are certainly not arguing that collaboration is the main cause of plagiarism or sexual harassment, we cannot ignore the way these debates are surfacing at the same time that collaborative practices are becoming more common. The response to both of these crises has been an outpouring of university policy making. But, while these policies may punish the single transgression or protect the institution from liability, they do not necessarily address the pedagogical philosophies that inherently contribute to these debates. If we do not continue to develop collaborative theory and practice, we risk exclusive homoglossia in the academy, language that continues to be familiar only to those who have been privileged to cross the boundary line that makes the institutional powers distinct. But, unless we break the silence and critically examine the taboos of the academy, we will become further enmeshed in a hierarchy that limits rather than encourages communication. For this academic incest suggested by collaboration to be productive, we must take a closer look at the institutional structures into which it is being imported.

Notes

[1]See Lisa Ede and Andrea Lunsford's *Singular Texts/Plural Authors: Perspectives on Collaborative Writing.*

[2]See W. Ross Winterowd's *A Teacher's Introduction to the Rhetorical Tradition in Composition.*

[3]Peter Elbow's *Writing Without Teachers* encourages the use of groups for peer response, but it's not a dialogue. The writer reads her work, then listens without comment as the readers respond individually.

[4]See H.I. Marrou's *A History of Education in Antiquity,* Chapter III.

[5]See Gerald Graff's *Beyond the Culture Wars.* In Chapter Four he insists, "Nobody is born knowing how to talk and write Intellectualspeak. By what process do we imagine students will acquire this language?" (75).

[6]See David Bartholomae's "Inventing the University."

[7]See Cynthia Tuell's "Composition Teaching as 'Women's Work': Daughters, Handmaids, Whores, and Mothers," and Elisabeth Daumer and Sandra Runzo's "Transforming the Composition Classroom."

[8]Recall the language commonly used to refer to writing centers as writing clinics and writing labs. While the doctor-patient metaphor is not present in composition theory, it is common for composition instructors to use language that suggests their emphasis in teaching is on symptoms (e.g., surface-level issues such as punctuation, grammar, and language interference, not global issues such as claims and support). See further George Hillock's *Research on Written Composition: New Directions for Teaching.*

[9]See Paulo Freire's *Pedagogy of the Oppressed.*

[10]See M.F. Belenky, B.M. Clinchy, N.R. Goldberger, and J.M. Tarule's *Women's Ways of Knowing: The Development of Self, Voice, and Mind.* Chapter 10.

[11]See George Lakoff and Mark Johnson's *Metaphors We Live By.*

[12]See Andrea A. Lunsford's "Intellectual Property, Concepts of Selfhood, and the Teaching of Writing."

[13]Bruce Appleby's presentation at CCCC (1993) discussed universities' multiple definitions of sexual harassment and the policies implemented to uphold respective definitions.

Works Cited

Appleby, Bruce C. "The Background on and Definitions of Sexual Harassment." The Rhetoric of Sexual Harassment. CCCC. San Diego, 1 Apr. 1993.

Bakhtin, M.M. "Discourse in the Novel." *The Dialogic Imagination.* Ed. Michael Holquist. Trans. Caryl Emerson and Michael Holquist. Austin: U of Texas P, 1981. 259-422.

Bartholomae, David. "Inventing the University." *When a Writer Can't Write.* Ed. Mike Rose. New York: Guilford, 1985. 134-65.

Belenky, M.F., B.M. Clinchy, N.R. Goldberger, and J.M. Tarule. *Women's Ways of Knowing: The Development of Self, Voice, and Mind.* New York: Basic, 1986.

Berthoff, Ann E. *The Making of Meaning: Metaphors, Models, and Maxims for Writing Teachers.* Portsmouth: Boynton/Cook, 1981.

Campbell, Karlyn Kohrs. *Man Cannot Speak for Her*. 2 vols. New York: Praeger, 1989.

Coles, William. *The Plural I—And After*. Portsmouth: Boynton/Cook, 1988.

Daumer, Elisabeth and Sandra Runzo. "Transforming the Composition Classroom." *Teaching Writing: Pedagogy, Gender and Equity*. Ed. Cynthia Caywood and Gilian Overing. Albany: SUNY P, 1987. 45-64.

Ede, Lisa, and Andrea A. Lunsford. *Singular Texts/Plural Authors: Perspectives on Collaborative Writing*. Carbondale: Southern Illinois UP, 1990.

Elbow, Peter. *Writing Without Teachers*. Oxford UP: New York, 1973.

Freire, Paulo. *Pedagogy of the Oppressed*. New York: Seabury, 1970.

Graff, Gerald. *Beyond the Culture Wars: How Teaching the Conflicts Can Revitalize American Education*. New York: Norton, 1992.

Heilker, Paul. "Nothing Personal: Twenty-Five Forays Into the Personal in (My) Composition Pedagogy." *The Writing Instructor* 12.2 (1993): 55-65.

Hillocks, George, Jr. *Research on Written Composition: New Directions for Teaching*. New York: National Conference on Research in English, 1988.

Lakoff George and Mark Johnson. *Metaphors We Live By*. Chicago: U of Chicago P, 1980.

Lunsford, Andrea A. "Intellectual Property, Concepts of Selfhood, and the Teaching of Writing." *The Writing Instructor* 12.2 (1993): 67-77.

Marrou, H.I. *A History of Education in Antiquity*. 1948. Trans. George Lamb. Madison: U of Wisconsin P, 1982.

Miller, Susan. "The Sad Women in the Basement: Images of Composition Teaching." *Textual Carnivals: The Politics of Composition*. Carbondale: Southern Illinois UP, 1991. 121-41.

Plato. *Phaedrus*. *The Rhetorical Tradition: Readings from Classical Times to the Present*. Ed. Patricia Bizzel and Bruce Herzberg. New York: St. Martin's, 1990. 113-43.

Tuell, Cynthia. "Composition as 'Women's Work': Daughters, Handmaids, Whores, and Mothers." *Writing Ourselves into the Story: Unheard Voices from Composition Studies*. Ed. Sheryl Fontaine and Susan Hunter. Carbondale: Southern Illinois UP, 1993.

Winkler, Anthony C., and Jo Ray McCuen. *The Journal Reader*. San Diego: Harcourt, 1993.

Winterowd, W. Ross, with Jack Blum. *A Teacher's Introduction to the Rhetorical Tradition in Composition*. Urbana: NCTE, 1994.

Woolf, Virginia. *A Room of One's Own*. San Diego: Harcourt, 1929.

Giving Birth to Voice:
The Professional Writing Tutor
as Midwife

Donna Fontanarose Rabuck
University of Arizona

In "The Transformation of Silence into Language and Action," Audre Lorde concludes, "... it is not difference which immobilizes us, but silence. And there are so many silences to be broken" (44). Lorde's words establish the parameters for my discussion of a tutoring program at the University of Arizona that has, for 14 years, been helping students who have often felt mute to break their silences and to give birth to their own unique voices with the help of professional tutors.

The Writing Skills Improvement Program (WSIP), the oldest and largest academic support program on the University of Arizona campus, was created in 1980 to assure minority and economically disadvantaged students of equal access to education. At that time, these students comprised the bulk of the Freshman Composition attrition rate. Often, when minority students received low grades on papers in writing classes, they felt disenfranchised, unheard, incapable of expression. Many of them question whether they really belong at the university. Minority students not only fail composition classes in alarming numbers, but drop out of class or, as is the case with many Native American students, leave the university altogether. Through a presidential initiative, Roseann Dueñas Gonzalez, the Assistant Director of Composition at the time (and now the first Chicana full professor), was charged to create a program that would enable these students to achieve academic success, to bridge the gap between the little writing these students often practiced in high school with the sophisticated writing they were expected to produce in college.

The Writing Skills Improvement Program, an independent writing center funded to serve a specific population of students, offers a model of sustained, individual professional tutoring. Our staff is comprised entirely of teachers and writers who hold Master's or Ph.D. degrees in English, ESL, or related disciplines. These tutors meet consistently with their students once or twice a week in hour-long sessions for the entire semester as students complete composition or writing-related classes. Our professional tutors provide culturally diverse students with an alternative model of education within the academy, a model that has ensured not only successful completion of writing classes, but also matriculation for a majority of this population.

The metaphor that most accurately conveys the role of the professional tutor is that of a midwife teacher. Writers such as Plato, Nietzsche, Freire, and a number of feminist scholars have explored this concept. In the last chapter of *Women's Ways of Knowing*, Mary Belenky and her coauthors define midwife teachers as being the opposite of what Freire considers "banker" teachers (53). They note,

> While the bankers deposit knowledge in the learner's head, the midwives draw it out. They assist the students in giving birth to their own ideas, in making their own tacit knowledge explicit and elaborating on it. (217)

This quotation describes exactly what professional tutors do. They draw out, assist, enable students to express ideas that are locked inside, thoughts that often exist at the borders of language itself. Central to our concept of midwife tutoring is the belief that giving birth to voice is a natural process; it is the tutor's role to use his or her professional expertise to nurture and encourage this growth.

In contrast to doctors within the medical hierarchy who tend to view birth as a product, an isolated event that results in a child, midwives view birth as a normal, healthy process not dependent on heavy intervention or extreme mechanical manipulation. While most doctors see pregnant women for brief periods of time and rely on scientific information to chart their progress, midwives tend to devote more time to talking with pregnant women, asking and answering questions that have to do with mental as well as physical health, finding out what their clients need to know, and providing information in language they can understand. Midwives treat each client as a particular individual whose pregnancy is unique (Flint 25). They spend consistent, sustained time offering advice, assurance, knowledge, and resources appropriate to each woman's needs at every stage of her pregnancy and birth.

The midwife tutor performs a similar function. Just as a contemporary midwife relies on years of training and extensive knowledge of the birthing process, so does a professional midwife tutor draw on resources as a teacher and writer—his or her own extensive knowledge of the writing process—and employ them in collaborative sessions with the student. The model is a holistic one based on the relationship that develops between the two over time as they sit side by side every week and talk—about life, language, the writing process, and the student's progress in the course and in school in general.

Like midwives, professional midwife tutors are sensitive to the social, political, and emotional factors that affect birth. When the tutor and student meet, the tutor gathers essential information about the student—what his or her educational background is, how prepared or unprepared s/he is in writing, what gaps in learning the student might have, what special needs must be addressed. Looking at the syllabus for the class, talking with the teacher (our tutors have telephone conversations and three-way conferences with teachers of composition classes), the tutor essentially develops a student-centered course of study designed to take the student to the next level of critical thinking and written expression. This development is process rather than product (grade) oriented, although we have found that sustained individual tutoring most often does result in higher grades in writing courses and in an increase in self-confidence in minority and economically disadvantaged writers.

One of the most crucial roles a midwife tutor plays is that of becoming a translator of the language and expectations of the class, of the teacher, and, indeed, of academic discourse itself. A number of the students we serve have not had as many opportunities to write or even speak English, so the language of the academy is often regarded as an alien discourse. We ask students to fill out background information sheets and have found that, although maybe 25% are more traditional ESL speakers, another 50% are first-generation college students who come from homes in which another language is spoken with the family. Therefore, the students don't have as many linguistic or literary resources to draw upon, nor as much facility with the English language as majority students. They are often reluctant to speak up in class and to ask for further explanation. And, since the majority of students we serve are completing composition classes taught primarily by graduate teaching assistants, the teachers themselves may have neither the experience nor the expertise to anticipate and provide the information these students need. Therefore, it is the professional midwife tutor who is qualified to supply what Mike Rose calls "background knowledge" to minority students in "comprehensible ways" (187). To do so, the tutor acts as a translator in a number of different contexts.

Many times the translating a tutor does occurs at the sentence level. As Judith Powers notes in "Rethinking Writing Center Conferencing Strategies for the ESL Writer," techniques that work well for majority students, such as answering a question with a question and refusing to mark up a draft, often do not address crucial concerns of ESL writers (40). I would add that the same is often true for minority writers. Our students have very real questions of usage that it is the tutor's job to answer, to point out in the drafts, and to work on with the student within the context of a paper. One of our tutors worked with an Apache student who showed her past attempts at writing with failing grades and teacher comments such as "Unreadable" and "Makes no grammatical sense." To this student, English was, as his tutor put it, "a strangely encoded language which shut him out." As the tutor and student got to know one another and discussed his first language, it became clear that Apache was structured syntactically the reverse of English. Once the tutor understood how sentences were constructed in the student's native language, she could teach him what he needed to know about sentence construction in English and alert him to problems of usage in his writing. Together, the tutor and student worked at the sentence level, discussing the differences in meaning that such reversal caused. They decided that this student needed to allow extra time in his writing process for revision at the sentence level. With time, encouragement and practice, he was able to express his excellent ideas in language that his teachers could understand.

Other times the tutor performs what I'd call cultural translation. For example, a Vietnamese student asked to write about the symbolism of the apple in James Joyce's "Araby" was understandably confused. Because she grew up in an Eastern culture, the Christian overlay of symbolism was lost to her. In this case, the tutor, as cultural translator, needed to provide information about Adam and Eve, the Old Testament, and the Christian religion. After providing a history for the student, the tutor encouraged her to think of and discuss a symbolic analogy from her own culture; after their discussion, the student had the information she needed to approach and complete the assignment.

Cultural translation often includes translating the rhetorical conventions of academic writing in English. Not only transitional ESL writers, but many minority writers are more familiar with rhetorics quite different from academic English. For example, Hispanic students may use flowery, elaborate prose that, while acceptable and encouraged in their "home" language, will often be called "wordy" and "repetitious" by their composition teacher. Korean writers, addressing mature audiences of their peers, often imply, more than they explicitly delineate, their ideas and leave readers to draw their own conclusions. In academic writing in English, however, teachers expect more clearly detailed information with explicit conclusions drawn from a body of evidence. Therefore, a crucial act of translation the tutor performs is to inform students of what academic expectations are and to show them how to provide the information their audiences expect.

Most often the translation a tutor performs is to phrase the assignment in terms the student can comprehend. For example, both English 101 and 102 classes at the University of Arizona include a unit on rhetorical analysis. This term itself is confusing to many students (as it is to many new graduate teaching assistants themselves). The tutor translates this technical language into terms the student can understand and demystifies the language in which the assignment is couched, thereby leading the student to find a way into the assignment rather than being shut out by unfamiliar terminology. Whereas within the institutional hierarchy a doctor (or a "banker teacher") may repeat the same technical information to a number of different clients regardless of their familiarity with the language, the midwife tutor as translator is sensitive to the needs of the person receiving the information and translates information at the level the student can best understand and work with.

One of the tutor's most important acts of translation is helping the student find a way to write his or her personal "story" into the context of an assignment for a composition class. Many minority and economically disadvantaged students are reticent to discuss their cultural background; they think it is something they have to leave behind when they come to college. However, as Roseann Gonzalez notes, "Every student possesses a body of folk knowledge ready to be tapped and formed into written discourse" (23). In this context, the midwife tutor as translator suggests ways the student can use knowledge s/he already possesses to satisfy the requirements of an essay. Because the midwife tutor and student develop a close relationship sustained over time, tutoring sessions often serve as holding spaces for personal narrative, safe spaces in which students speak in their own voices about what really matters to them. The midwife tutor as translator does not see such discussion of personal, cultural, and social story as outside of or at the margins of relationship, but central to it. Thus, s/he recognizes that, if students don't have a chance to explore and express their story, they can't really give birth to an authentic, engaged, individual voice that expresses the fullness of who they are. The tutor as translator can suggest ways the student can write about his or her culture, thereby linking private and public worlds, head and heart, home and school (if and only if the student is comfortable doing this). Students are thereby empowered to enter into the conversation of an academic discourse community in which learning is truly a reciprocal process.

Another significant role the professional midwife tutor plays is that of a mentor, guiding the student through the process of composition, through the course, often through the university itself. The tutor knows of other departments and services on campus and can connect students with the Department of African American Studies, the Poetry Center, academic and peer advisors. S/he can suggest literary resources, writers to read, readings to attend, all that lies at the intersection of the student's culture and the institution. Most importantly, like the professional midwife who guides the client through the process of gestation, labor, and delivery, the midwife tutor as mentor is an experienced guide through the process of writing, one who believes that giving birth to voice is a natural process that occurs when the student has all the information s/he needs, feels safe, has connected with the task at hand, and has had the task translated into terms s/he understands. The midwife tutor as mentor provides a learning experience, an environment, and an ongoing conversation that encourages growth. Research has shown mentors to exert a powerful influence on minority youth, yet there are few minority faculty members on campus and they are often overworked themselves. In the absence of a cadre of professional tutors who are themselves minority teachers, a midwife tutor respectful of and knowledgeable about the writing and culture of the student is an invaluable resource.

And what of the place of the professional tutor within the university? It is much like that of a midwife. Misunderstood by many, marginal in the institutional hierarchy, professional tutors often experience lack of respect within the academy itself. At the University of Arizona, our staff members make very little, averaging $8.00 an hour, and teach at community colleges at night or do freelance writing to help support themselves, just as midwives often work as nurses to supplement their income. There are more lucrative jobs and they have the expertise for them, but tutoring, like midwifery, is a choice, a vocation. When graduate students tutor for a semester during one of our summer programs, their experiences inevitably lead them to become better teachers. And who are the writers and teachers who are attracted to our program in the first place? Midwife teachers, teachers comfortable with the conferencing method of teaching that Donald Murray details so well in *A Writer Teaches Writing*; teachers who see themselves as collaborators in their students' learning process but are tired of lack of support for excellence in teaching or of the authority role they often are forced to assume in the classroom. These are people who feel that the real work is sitting next to the student, week after week, "with" the student, just as a midwife is "mid," "with" her client at every step of the process. Like Barbara McClintock, the Nobel prize-winning scientist quoted by poet Linda Hogan as "listening to what the corn spoke to her" (77), they prefer to hear other voices besides their own, to learn as much as they teach, to respect the individuality of the student whose voice they will assist in giving birth. They engage in what some have called a more maternal process of teaching, a relationship that develops and persists over time. In fact, when students return after a semester and request the same tutor again, we are happy to comply, knowing that their conversation will go on to another level as the student prepares for the Upper Division Writing Proficiency Exam, an advanced literature class, or the writing emphasis class for his or her major. In an institution in which faces, names, and classes constantly change, the consistency of the tutor-student relationship, if desired, can make a big difference in the academic lives and careers of minority and economically disadvantaged students.

Enough theory. What about results? Before the establishment of the program, minority students comprised the bulk of the composition attrition rate. Now that the majority of these students are served by us, 99% of WSIP students pass their English courses; an average of 65% improve their beginning grade by 1 grade level; 30% improve by 2 grades; and 2% improve by three grades. Students enrolled in the program have gone on to win first and second prizes in the Freshman Composition Essay Contest and to have their essays published in *A Student's Guide to Freshman Composition*, a required text that is published yearly. Participating students have also won awards for Outstanding Undergraduate Students, Outstanding Minority Students, have placed into honors English classes, and have received an array of academic honors.

In 1992, the College of Arts and Sciences presented the Writing Skills Improvement Program with an Award for Excellence in Minority Education. Our program and our tutors were credited with improving the writing and retention of over 15,000 students in workshops and tutorials since the program's inception. Now the figures are well over 16,000 and the number of minority students we serve in individual sessions totals about 6,000, averaging 600-800 yearly.

Writing Skills was the first support program on campus to conduct an accountability study (1986) to measure objectively the quality of our services. This study tracked participants and nonparticipants for five years. The results indicated that professional tutoring not only improves student's writing skills but their academic skills in general. The average participants' English course grades before and after tutoring evidenced a difference of 1.37 grade points. In addition, the mean GPA of participants was .91 points above that of nonparticipants. Overall, Writing Skills students earned higher grades and were eligible to graduate, in contrast to only 53% of the nonparticipants. The accountability study proved that, not only does our model of professional midwife tutoring enable minority students to pass and excel in composition classes, it also improves students' overall academic performance and ensures their persistence toward graduation.

These days it is "politically correct" to talk about and attempt to address the needs of this population of students. However, when we began 14 years ago, we had to prove that a land grant institution such as the University of Arizona needed to demonstrate a real commitment to the minority peoples who will, by the year 2000, comprise a majority of the school-age population in the state. Our commitment and our methods haven't changed, but what has become clear is that midwife tutoring, this model of professional, sustained, individual writing assistance, is a vital and effective tool in ensuring equal access to education for minority and economically disadvantaged students. It is a model that needs to be incorporated into other writing centers and academic support programs.

There is a growing awareness on the part of writing centers that ESL students have different needs than majority students. I believe that this is true for many minority students as well. Luckily, at the University of Arizona, our students have a choice. We have a writing center staffed by peer tutors that is free and open to everyone, and we have the Writing Skills Improvement Program for students who wish to commit themselves to the development of what might be a hitherto unheard voice. And we have midwife tutors who are there to assist them, knowing that what resides inside of them is worth drawing out, is revolutionary, is a silence that needs to be broken.[1]

Notes

[1]Thanks to Valentina Abordonado and Duane Roen for sharing their unpublished article, "The Writing Teacher as Midwife," with me.

Works Cited

Belenky, Mary Field, Blythe McVicker Clinchy, Nancy Rule Goldberger, and Jill Mattuck Tarule. *Women's Ways of Knowing: The Development of Self, Voice, and Mind*. New York: Basic, 1986.

Flint, Caroline. "On the Brink: Midwifery in Britain." *The Midwife Challenge*. Ed. Sheila Kitzinger. London: Pandora, 1988. 22-39.

Freire, Paulo. *Pedagogy of the Oppressed*. Trans. Myra Bergman Ramos. New York: Continuum, 1993.

Gonzalez, Roseann Dueñas. "Teaching Mexican American Students to Write: Capitalizing on the Culture." *English Journal* November 1982: 20-24.

Gonzalez, Roseann Dueñas, and Donna Fontanarose Rabuck. "Writing Skills Improvement Program Accountability Study." Unpublished Report, April 1986, University of Arizona.

Hogan, Linda. "Hearing Voices." *The Writer on Her Work* Vol. 2. Ed. Janet Sternberg. New York: Norton, 1991. 77-81.

Lorde, Audre. *Sister Outsider*. Freedom: Crossing, 1984.

Murray, Donald. *A Writer Teaches Writing*. 2nd ed. Boston: Houghton, 1988.

Powers, Judith K. "Rethinking Writing Center Conferencing Strategies for the ESL Writer." *The Writing Center Journal* 13.2 (1993): 39-47.

Rose, Mike. *Lives on the Boundary*. New York: Penguin, 1989.

Writing Centers as Sites for Writing Transfer Research

Julie Hagemann
Purdue University Calumet

As a writing teacher, I am especially concerned with how students learn academic discourse. I want to give my students as complex a view of academic reading and writing as I can because I am charged with "initiating" them into the academic discourse community, to use Patricia Bizzell's way of characterizing composition classes. If I want to be honest to that charge, I have to somehow account for multiple versions of academic language conventions. Therein lies the dilemma: while I, as an English teacher, am constrained by my own disciplinary training and departmental course curriculum, my students must sign up for a vast range of courses in departments all over campus to fulfill their liberal arts requirements. While I am teaching the conventions of English discourse, they may also be writing history or anthropology papers or biology lab reports. David Bartholomae is one composition specialist who recognizes that undergraduates are asked to learn a complex set of rules—and to learn them all at once. He says in "Inventing the University" that

> [e]very time a student sits down to write for us, he has to invent the university for the occasion—invent the university, that is, or a branch of it, like History or Anthropology or Economics or English. He has to learn to speak our language, to speak as we do, to try on the peculiar ways of knowing, selecting, evaluating, reporting, concluding, and arguing that define the discourse of our community. Or perhaps I should say the *various* discourses of our community, since it is in the nature of a liberal arts education that a student, [in] the first year or two, must learn to try on a variety of voices and interpretive schemes—to write, for example, as a literary critic one day and an experimental psychologist the next .... [Moreover,] speaking and writing will most certainly be required long before the skill is "learned." And this, understandably, causes problems. (273; emphasis in the original)

Bartholomae's description encourages us to think about how students might use their many literacy experiences to learn to write. Recent studies have attempted to address the connection between composition and other disciplinary courses, but I argue that they are limited in scope because they are classroom based (cf. Anderson et al.; Chiseri-Strater; McCarthy). These recent studies have focused, in particular, on the ways undergraduates transfer skills from one course to another; the consensus is that transfer is problematic. In short, these studies fail to substantiate the long-held assumption that skills from English courses will transfer easily to other courses. For example, Lucille McCarthy found in "A Stranger in Strange Lands" that her student did not make an easy transfer from his first-year English course to biology because he was so over-whelmed with the technical language of the journal articles he was to summarize that he completely forgot he knew how to summarize successfully. Moreover, Susan Miller in "Cross-Curricular Underlife" (Anderson et al.) and Elizabeth Chiseri-Strater in *Academic Literacies* found the writing environment in their students' non-English classes was so different from that in their English courses that they were unable to transfer skills because they could not replicate the context on their own. While their English teachers were careful to model the writing process in small classes with lots of time for personal attention to each student, the non-English teachers assigned papers to their large classes and left the students on their own. All three studies suggest that students do not easily transfer writing strategies from their composition class to assignments in other courses.

It is interesting to note that none of these studies refers to writing centers or a possible contribution tutors might have made to the students' understanding of the assignment or of academic discourse in general, thus improving their ability to transfer skills learned in composition to their other courses. Rather, all of these studies are based in self-contained classrooms. Moreover, as valuable as these studies are, they tend to focus on what I call "diachronic writing transfer"; that is, they focus on following a small number of students through their English composition class one semester and through a disciplinary course the second semester. McCarthy and Chiseri-Strater follow students through a semester of composition and a subsequent semester of biology, art history and political science. Miller meets her students in a composition course fall quarter, and, although she asks them to keep a journal for all their classes the second quarter, she does not attempt to describe how the learning in one class impacts on other courses taken that same quarter.

While these studies give us important insights into the problematic claim that students transfer writing skills from their English composition course to courses in other disciplines, these studies are in fact limited because they are classroom based. They give too simplistic a view of the context in which undergraduates are forced to learn academic literacy because they look at one discipline at a time. Full-time undergraduates must juggle four or five classes each school term and must figure out which of their many literacy experiences can be brought to bear each time they sit down to write an assignment in any of their classes (Popken). As a result, current studies in writing transfer do not address the problem that I am concerned with—namely, that first-year students must learn a number of academic discourses simultaneously and that each learning experience has some impact on subsequent ones. I call this "synchronic writing transfer."

In these theorists' defense, I grant that such classroom-based inquiry is detailed and time-consuming, and to add the complex dimension of synchronic transfer is to add to an already difficult method of research. Nevertheless, if we are to get a more accurate picture of how undergraduates learn to write, we have to study their synchronous, that is, simultaneous, experiences. In short, we need to focus our research on our students' interdisciplinary writing transfer. Because this new focus is difficult in a classroom, which by definition is tied to a specific discipline, we need to relocate our research to an interdisciplinary site—the writing center, particularly one that has a campus-wide mission. Anecdotal evidence suggests that a writing center tutor often has a broader view of a student's writing than any one of his teachers. It is often true that, once a student is introduced to the writing center and finds the tutor's advice helpful, he comes back for help on all his papers. Hence, the writing center tutor often helps in assignments for all of his classes. This unique quality of the writing center makes it the ideal place for research into synchronous writing transfer.

I want to turn now to a concrete example of the kind of writing center-based research I am calling for. It is the story of the struggles of an inexperienced undergraduate, whom I will call Lih Mei, to negotiate writing tasks in five courses representing three disciplines, a story that emerges from tutor records dated fall 1991 at Writing Tutorial Services, a campus-wide writing center, at Indiana University in Bloomington. It is a serendipitous study because I happened onto it; it was not systematically designed nor were data systematically collected. As a result, even though the record narratives are extensive, there are many details missing—including any writing samples from Lih Mei that might allow us to see with our own eyes the observations reported by various tutors who worked with her. Although we must treat this story with a great deal of caution, there is something equally compelling in Lih Mei's experience to point to the potential of writing centers as sites for synchronous writing transfer research and for the potential this research has in giving us an understanding of how undergraduates learn to write academic prose.

Lih Mei was a fifth-year senior from Taiwan majoring in economics. The record for her first visit reports that she had finished all of her economics courses and was taking electives to fill out graduation requirements. Because her sister was a leisure services major, Lih Mei thought she would take several recreation courses herself and enrolled in three courses in the Health/Physical Education/Recreation department: "Recreation and Leisure" (R&L), "Tourism and Commercial Recreation" (T&CR), and "Leisure and Aging" (L&A). The faculty in this department had enthusiastically embraced writing-across-the-curriculum and usually assigned weekly or biweekly microthemes, one- to two-page pieces of writing that asked students to work with the concepts they were studying. Over 80 percent of Lih Mei's visits were motivated by these leisure services classes. She also signed up for a course titled "China: The Enduring Heritage," a course in the East Asian Languages and Literatures department that fulfills an undergraduate's cultural studies requirement; later, however, after earning a failing grade on her first paper and a personality conflict with her teacher, she decided to drop the course. Finally, she signed up for "Introduction to Philosophy" in the philosophy department. She had to write two short papers for this class based on texts provided by the professor, but Lih Mei was sent to the graduate assistant assigned to the course for help with these papers because the writing center tutors felt uncomfortable giving advice on readings they could not comprehend well.

The initial record notes that Lih Mei said she had never learned to write because no one had ever held her accountable for clear, well-argued prose in her own words. When she had to write in her economics classes, the records said she claimed, her professors got the gist of her meaning and gave her credit for that. While it certainly may be true that Lih Mei's economics professors did not spend much class time talking explicitly about how to write, it is also possible that Lih Mei may not have been able to summon whatever rhetorical knowledge she did have in the face of a new discipline she was only casually familiar with. Just as McCarthy's student felt so overwhelmed by the content knowledge of his biology class that he could not summon his strategies for summarizing, Lih Mei may have felt lost and unprepared in spite of previous training in writing.

I have compiled a summary of Lih Mei's many visits, taken from accounts of the tutorials (See Appendix). This timeline makes evident the sheer number of Lih Mei's—sometimes daily—visits (44) and individual writing assignments (19 or 20) as well as the dizzying range of roles she had to negotiate, sometimes simultaneously, as she worked on several papers at once—roles of text processor, decision-maker, debater, counselor and researcher. Although a number of the visits were devoted to work on grammar and mechanics, especially at the end of the semester when she had two lengthy research papers to finish, the bulk of her visits were devoted to talk about the roles she was expected to play and about the kind of authoritative presence she should assume in her texts. I want to highlight some of these visits to discuss the ways that Lih Mei gradually learned to more successfully negotiate these various expectations, learning what rhetorical strategies she could and could not transfer.

As a framework for my analysis, I want to draw on Barbara Walvoord and Lucille McCarthy's *Thinking and Writing in College,* a book I found especially helpful in articulating the kind of advice I saw recorded in the various accounts of tutor sessions. As the subtitle suggests, Walvoord and McCarthy's book is a naturalistic study of students in courses in four different disciplines: Business Management, Western Civilization, Human Sexuality and Biological Literature. Walvoord and McCarthy conclude that most of the assignments they analyzed asked students to write in the role of "professional-in-training," expecting students not merely to process their text and lecture notes but to use those notes in some kind of professional capacity. The students were expected not just to comprehend the material but to synthesize and apply it. However, they also noted that a "professional-in-training" role meant a different set of tasks in each class. Business students were asked to develop business plans and use texts in their rationales (the role of decision-maker). The Western Civilization professor, on the other hand, encouraged his students to learn to debate, to engage texts in a kind of dialogue, arguing with and against them (the role of debater). The major writing assignment in the Human Sexuality class asked students to act in the role of counselor, to raise a number of options, but not to settle on one, just as in the counseling situation, where the final decision is left in the hands of those counseled (the role of counselor). Biology students focused on the role of scientist, especially in developing operational definitions that could be quantitatively researched (the role of researcher). Walvoord and McCarthy emphasize again and again in their book that teachers across disciplines share the broad concern of training students to, for example, name problems, devise definitions, seek options, build rationale, argue positions, in order to help them develop as professionals—though these take different forms in different disciplines. These are the rhetorical functions that undergraduates must try on in the process of learning academic discourse (Bartholomae).

These are also the roles that Lih Mei was asked to assume in her many microthemes and writing assignments. Let me come back to the timeline and point out some key moments in Lih Mei's process of negotiating various disciplinary expectations and of learning what rhetorical moves she could and could not transfer. She begins first with a summary for her Leisure and Aging class. This is a familiar kind of assignment for most students, one that requires them to process a reading and reproduce its main points in their own text. Lih Mei responded effortlessly by accurately summarizing it. The fact that she could complete the assignment with such a degree of success indicates that she was probably fairly familiar with processing and summarizing text and that she wisely drew on that experience. In this instance, she seemed to easily transfer knowledge she learned in the past to this new writing task.

However, she was not as successful with her second assignment, this one for Tourism and Commercial Recreation. Her assignment sheet asked her to read an article and to devise a plan to develop tourism on a Native American reservation in the Southwest that did not exploit the Native Americans. The records show that in this assignment, Lih Mei first faced the realities of varying expectations; she first came to see from her tutor's reaction to her draft that she could not simply transfer her summarizing experiences to this new task. She had once again assumed the same role of text processor but that proved to be inappropriate. Although she had accurately identified the main ideas of the article and summarized them, she made no mention of a plan. Text processing is different from decision making in part by the way texts are used. Text processing focuses on points from the text, usually in the order the author presents them. In decision making, on the other hand, texts serve the dual function of giving students both ideas for a solution and the supporting details for a rationale for that plan (Walvoord and McCarthy). The tutor notes she showed Lih Mei how to mine her texts for ideas and reasons to devise and justify her plan. That is, Lih Mei needed to learn how to extract data from a text to support her ideas.

By the time that Lih Mei was asked to devise another plan on October 2nd—this time for Recreation and Leisure—she knew how to assume the role of decision-maker. The assignment this time was to suggest to a busy executive ways to relax. The tutorial record notes that this draft was the best she had written to date. However, she was still having trouble building a rationale for her plan. While Lih Mei could identify what she felt was a "good" recreation plan for a busy Taiwanese executive, she was not yet able to successfully argue why he should adopt it. She was much more assertive with her own ideas, much less tied to the text, but she still did not know how to justify her advice. The tutor used the hour to help Lih Mei explain why she had recommended the activities she had. Because Lih Mei had so many microthemes and assignments in which she was expected to assume the role of decision-maker or counselor, helping her think through the different components of that role proved to be an essential move toward creating independence in Lih Mei. She was learning to judge when that rhetorical role was called for and what skills she needed to bring to bear as she approached a new assignment.

The role that Lih Mei seemed to have the most trouble assuming was the role of debater in dialogue with the text. In her October 8th microtheme, she was asked to take a stand on the following statement for her Leisure and Aging class: "The 'Busy Ethic' does/does not legitimate retirement for individuals and society." As the timeline suggests, this is a difficult task for Lih Mei because it takes four visits for her to polish this one-page paper. To respond to this assignment successfully, Lih Mei needed to extract the author's definition of "busy ethic," take a stand on whether it legitimated retirement, and build a rationale for her stand by using or disputing the author's points. Debating is different from decision making in its use of text. In decision making, a writer extracts information to support her ideas, while in debating she focuses on the text, isolating key points to discuss. Rather than a gold mine of facts, the text functions as a turn-of-talk that Lih Mei must listen and respond to in order to keep the "conversation" going (Walvoord and McCarthy).

The first visit was a brainstorming session because, the record says, Lih Mei had no idea how to begin. Apparently, she recognized that she had no previous successful experiences to draw on in doing this new assignment. She had had two earlier assignments that used texts in this way, but they were not successful. She had earned a failing grade on an earlier analysis of an Ancient Chinese short story for her Chinese Heritage class, and, according to the records, the texts in her philosophy class so completely baffled Lih Mei and the writing center tutor that she was encouraged to seek help from the graduate assistant assigned to the course. To help her address the "Busy Ethic" assignment, the tutor talked with Lih Mei about what it meant to take a stand. When she came back with her first draft, Lih Mei was able to take a stand, but her rationale did not make explicit use of the text she was responding to. She did not know to, or know *how* to, acknowledge her paper was part of a conversation of texts. It took another draft to begin to make her monologue about the legitimacy of retirement into a dialogue with a particular text.

Space constrains me from telling more of this story of an undergraduate learning how to negotiate a range of conflicting expectations in her quest to learn academic literacy. It might be said that Lih Mei is not a typical case because she is an international student and because she had so many writing assignments in one semester. Granted, Lih Mei comes from a culture that does not seem to value the same kind of "professional-in-training" literacy that her American teachers expected, which indeed may account to some degree for her struggle to assume an authoritative presence in her text (Shen; Matalene). But composition theorists, David Bartholomae and Michael Carter in particular, argue that traditional American students wrestle with this as well. They claim that all students need some time to learn to based their textual authority on content knowledge, as a professional would do. For this reason, I believe that Lih Mei is a typical undergraduate with typically uneven successes at knowing what rhetorical strategies to transfer.

As writing-across-the-curriculum takes hold, more and more students will be writing as much as Lih Mei. More and more students will be confronted with learning several academic discourses simultaneously. Although I have to be cautious, I am convinced Lih Mei's story suggests that undergraduates are faced with a complex task in learning to judge which of their varied writing experiences they can bring to bear on a new assignment and that writing centers are the ideal sites for studying how they do that.

Works Cited

Anderson, Worth, Cynthia Best, Alycia Black, John Hurst, Brandt Miller, and Susan Miller. "Cross-Curricular Underlife: A Collaborative Report on Ways with Academic Words." *College Composition and Communication* 41 (1990): 11-36.

Bartholomae, David. "Inventing the University." *When a Writer Can't Write: Studies in Writer's Block and Other Composing-Process Problems.* Ed. Mike Rose. New York: Guilford P, 1985. Excerpted in *Perspectives on Literacy.* Ed. Eugene Kintgen, Barry Kroll, and Mike Rose. Carbondale: Southern Illinois UP, 1988. 273-85.

Bizzell, Patricia. "College Composition: Initiation into the Academic Discourse Community." *Curriculum Inquiry* 12.2 (1982): 191-207.

Carter, Michael. "What is *Advanced* about Advanced Composition?" *Teaching Advanced Composition: Why and How.* Ed. Katherine H. Adams and John L. Adams. Portsmouth: Boynton/Cook, 1991.

Chiseri-Strater, Elizabeth. *Academic Literacies: The Public and Private Discourse of University Students.* Portsmouth: Boynton/Cook, 1991.

Matalene, Carolyn. "Contrastive Rhetoric: An American Writing Teacher in China." *College English* 47 (1985): 789-808.

McCarthy, Lucille. "A Stranger in Strange Lands." *Research in the Teaching of English* 21 (1987): 233-65.

Popken, Randall. "Genre Transfer in Developing Adult Writers." *Focuses* 5 (1992): 3-17.

Shen, Fen. "The Classroom and the Wider Culture: Identity as a Key to Learning English Composition." *College Composition and Communication* 40 (1989): 459-66.

Walvoord, Barbara E., and Lucille P. McCarthy. *Thinking and Writing in College: A Naturalistic Study of Students in Four Disciplines.* Urbana: NCTE, 1990.

Appendix
A Time Line of Lih Mei's Writing Center Visits[1]

Date		Course/Assignment[2]	Role
9/13	L&A	Summarize article: "The Leisure Experience"	Text processor
9/17	T&CR	Devise tourism plan for SW Indian reservation	Decision-maker—generate plan
9/18	T&CR	*SW Indian tourism plan	*Decision-maker
9/25	CEH	Analyze Ancient Chinese short story	Debater—analyze text
9/26	L&A	Letter to grandmother about diabetes	Counselor
9/27	PHIL	Argue to what extent humans have free will	Debater
9/30	PHIL	*Free will argument	Debater
10/01	PHIL	*Free will argument	*Debater
10/02	R&L	Devise recreation plan for busy executive	Counselor/Decision-maker—generate plan
10/03	TC&R	Graph data indicating effectiveness of 2 travel brochures	Decision-maker—analyze given data
10/07	R&L	*Recreation plan for executive	*Counselor/decision-maker

10/08	T&CR	*Brochure effectiveness graph	*Decision-maker
	L&A	(Dis)Agree "The busy ethic does/does not legitimate retirement"	Debater—engage text in dialogue
10/ 09	**L&A**	***Busy ethic argument**	***Debater**
10/10	T&CR	Devise plan to control visitors to Yosemite NP	Decision-maker—generate plan
10/11	**L&A**	***Busy ethic argument**	***Debater**
10/12	**L&A**	***Busy ethic argument**	***Debater**
10/14	TC&R	*Review travel book	Debater—evaluate text
10/18	TC&R	*Review of travel book	*Debater
10/30	R&L	Compare recreation before and after video boom	Researcher—find data and analyze
10/31	L&A	Argue from 8 given statements	Decision-maker—analyze given data
11/04	L&A	*8 statements argument	*Decision-maker
	TC&R	Write research paper (outdoor recreation facilities for elderly and disabled)	Researcher—find data and analyze
	TC&R	Devise marketing plan for recreation event (Chinese New Year party)	Decision-maker—generate plan

11/05	T&CR	*New Year marketing plan	*Decision-maker
11/06	T&CR	*New Year marketing plan	*Decision-maker
11/11	T&CR	*Research paper (outdoor rec)	*Researcher
11/12	L&A	Respond to letter-to-editor	Debater—engage text in dialogue
	T&CR	*New Year marketing plan	*Decision-maker
11/13	T&CR	*Research paper (outdoor rec)	*Researcher
11/18	L&A	Write research paper (health and fitness facilities for elderly	Researcher
11/19	L&A	*Response to letter-to-editor	*Debater
	T&CR	*Research paper (outdoor rec)	*Researcher
11/21	PHIL	Argue how opposing claims of holism and reductionism can be reconciled	Debater—analyze text
11/22	T&CR	*Research paper (outdoor rec)	*Researcher
11/25	T&CR	*Research paper (outdoor rec)	*Researcher
11/26	T&CR	*Research paper (outdoor rec)	*Researcher
12/02	L&A	*Response to letter-to-editor	*Debater
	T&CR	*Research paper (outdoor rec)	*Researcher
12/03	T&CR	Analyze two travel brochures for effectiveness	Decision-maker—analyze given data

12/04	T&CR	*Research paper (outdoor rec)	*Researcher
12/05	T&CR	*Research paper (outdoor rec)	*Researcher
12/06	T&CR	*Research paper (outdoor rec)	*Researcher
12/09	T&CR	*Research paper (outdoor rec)	*Researcher
12/10	L&A	*Research paper (health fac)	*Researcher
12/11		Record lost	
12/12		Record lost	
12/13	L&A	*Research paper (health fac)	*Researcher
	L&A	Write take-home exam (tell 4th-graders what it's like to grow old)	Counselor
12/16	L&A	*Take-home exam (4th-graders)	*Counselor
	L&A	*Research paper (health fac)	*Researcher
12/18	L&A	*Research paper (health fac)	*Researcher

---

[1] These visits were made Fall semester 1991 to Writing Tutorial Services, an interdisciplinary, campuswide writing center at Indiana University in Bloomington.

[2] Key: CEH = China, The Enduring Heritage
PHIL = An Introduction to Philosophy
R&L = Recreation and Leisure
T&CR = Tourism and Commercial Recreation
L&A = Leisure and Aging
*   = Indicates a subsequent visit for a givenassignment

Entries in **boldface** are discussed in detail in the text.

Holistic Scoring:
A Valuable Tool for Improving
Writing Across the Curriculum

Robert W. Holderer
Edinboro University of Pennsylvania

Students often are frustrated in composing discourse across the curriculum because they lack a clear idea of how to write for given academic audiences. Part of this problem comes from the perceptions students have of their classes. Many see no relationship between required courses and their educational goals and take classes because they are required to. As soon as they complete those requirements, they often leave the academic discipline, never to return. These students lack the motivation to learn how to write for a particular field other than to receive a "good grade." Other students see clear relationships between courses and their career goals, but they lack strategies to compose effective discourse. Only a few students in any given class can compose discourse fluently within a discipline or perceive relationships among seemingly unrelated disciplines. As a whole, students come to classes with significantly different composing abilities and attitudes toward developing those abilities. What gets lost is effective writing across the curriculum.

Faculty are likewise frustrated and often complain to English departments and writing centers about poor student writing; however, they frequently do not realize that they, too, are responsible for part of the poor writing their students produce. Too often they create assignments without assessing students' abilities to complete the cognitive tasks these assignments call for. Students frequently cannot synthesize unfamiliar material that seems unrelated to them; consequently, faculty receive numbers of papers consisting of little more than strings of regurgitated paraphrases and quotations rather than papers with thoughtful, original ideas. When analyzing discourse, faculty frequently lack strategies for communicating student weaknesses other than to categorize them through traditional grammatical labels. Rather than viewing poor writing as part of the student's cognitive inability to forge connections between unfamiliar and rather abstract ideas, faculty sometimes view convoluted ideas in terms of a student's ignorance of the rules of grammar and punctuation. Unfortunately, what instructors label "grammatical error" may point to the student's inability to synthesize material he or she does not fully grasp. Because many instructors lack strategies and vocabulary for evaluating writing constructively on a rhetorical level, they often conclude that students cannot write and subsequently abandon term papers and essay exams in favor of more "objective" methods of evaluation. The saddest part of this scenario is that most students do the bulk of their writing in their freshman composition classes, and few instructors across the curriculum strive to maintain and develop those skills. As a result, students do not develop critical thinking skills, which depend so much on clear writing.

The writing center can help overcome these problems by showing instructors how to design effective writing assignments and strategies for evaluating drafts—especially through the use of a scoring guide. Studies have shown that valid and reliable evaluations of writing can be obtained through analytic, primary trait, and holistic scoring methods when used with large-scale measures; however, research has yet to address the potential of these three methods for allowing instructors to diagnose writing in progress. If modified, these methods can greatly assist teachers in their efforts to elicit thoughtful discourse from students. A well-written scoring guide offers instructors a means for evaluating drafts clearly; it provides the writing center a solid referral form; and it gives students precise information to assist them in creating clear, focused papers.

To date, the three most popular methods for evaluating papers have been holistic, primary trait, and analytic scoring. Holistic scoring enables instructors to evaluate written discourse by general impression (White, 1985). Rather than allowing instructors to evaluate a text by judging its constituent parts, holistic scoring allows them to evaluate a piece of writing as a unit. With most holistic scoring procedures, faculty members write detailed scoring guides that give general characteristics describing writing that fits each numerical score on the scale (White, 1985). These characteristics can include rhetorical specifications, sentence structure, and usage. Holistic scoring has become popular because the assumptions behind it integrate well with those behind recent developments in linguistic, composition, and critical theory (Huot, 1990; White, 1985). It is also popular because it is the most economical of all direct writing procedures (Faigley et al., 1985; White, 1985). Faculty can also write a holistic scoring guide in such a way that it can be used for more than one assignment.

Primary trait scoring allows readers to identify one or more traits appropriate to a specific writing task, based on the assumption that the rhetorical situation pertinent to the writing assignment creates the criteria for evaluation (Lloyd-Jones, 1977). When instructors create a new assignment, they must also create a new guide as the rhetorical dimensions change with each new assignment. With each assignment, instructors will evaluate only those traits that emanate from the rhetorical situation created by the purpose and intended audience of the question itself and the particular content demands of the assignment (Huot, 1990). Because primary trait scoring focuses on those specific rhetorical features required by a given assignment, students who may normally compose proficient drafts will receive low scores if they do not specifically address those rhetorical features in a particular text (Dawe, 1990).

Analytic scoring allows instructors to focus on several qualities germane to good writing. Instructors give scores to individual, identifiable traits, and scores are tallied to provide the overall rating for the paper (Diederich, 1974). Diederich's (1974) original rubric used an interval scale from 1 to 5 to measure the following dimensions of writing: the quality of ideas; organization; wording; flavor; usage; punctuation; spelling; and handwriting. Other scales allow instructors to weigh qualities like content or organization more heavily than other traits (Huot, 1990). Analytic scoring takes longer for raters to evaluate, its criteria may be more appropriate for a final draft than one in progress, and, with the exception of straight grammatical considerations, it often correlates highly enough with holistic scoring to make some qualities seem redundant (Bauer, 1981; Freedman, 1981; White, 1985).

Up until now, research in the reliability and validity of all three scoring systems has addressed only large-scale assessments. Literature connecting these methods with classroom practice exists, but researchers have largely limited their use to validating the potential of new teaching methods through the traditional pre- and post-test. If instructors are indeed using these methods as part of actual classroom practice, they are not writing about it. A survey of scholarship reveals only three composition researchers—Paulis (1985) and Westcott and Gardner (1984)—who connect holistic scoring with lessons in revising papers, but they apparently limit its use to ranking drafts as a peer-critiquing activity. No literature exists linking any of the three methods with courses across the curriculum, strongly indicating that teachers in disciplines other than English are unaware of the benefits of using analytic, primary trait, or holistic scoring for evaluating writing.

The use of evaluating drafts with a scoring guide promises a number of key advantages, especially if instructors create guides that blend the best features of holistic, analytic, and primary trait scoring so that guides evolve beyond simple ranking instruments to ones that possess the ability to generate diagnostic information. First, if instructors create a scoring guide at the same time as the assignment itself, they will find that the guide will help them to focus on the goals of their assignment. The act of moving back and forth from assignment to scoring guide compels instructors to think in terms of those specific skills and strategies students will need for composing the given assignment. This deliberation helps instructors avoid the stacks of poorly written papers they often receive when they unintentionally create assignments without thinking of clear evaluation criteria in advance. As instructors create a scoring guide, they must clearly describe the traits of outstanding papers for top scores and anticipate specific pitfalls or panic points for the bottom scores. As they think of these pitfalls, they can revise the assignment to avoid them or plan class activities to guide students through them. As novices in creating a scoring guide, instructors will need significant help, which, in turn, affords the writing center an opportunity to serve everyone, not just "remedial students." Faculty can get first-hand exposure to the methods writing center personnel use with students. Most of all, the writing center can head off potential problems that can become frustrating for students at a later time. Collaboration between writing center staff and department faculty members helps everyone. Faculty can learn good strategies for teaching writing in a non-defensive manner, and the writing center gains a clearer idea of the standards that department faculty wish to impose.

Second, a scoring guide allows instructors to respond to writing in a quick and efficient manner. It works well for both instructors and students because the criteria for an "A" paper are made clear from the beginning, and faculty do not need to spend class time re-explaining assignments. Students have a clear idea of what is expected of them before they start researching and writing assignments, and, when instructors return submitted drafts, students have a tool that can provide them with precise revision strategies.

Third, a scoring guide also helps the writing center staff work effectively with students. The scores and highlighted comments from the scoring rubric become a type of referral sheet that allows writing center tutors to provide effective assistance quickly. Information provided by the scoring sheet is a time-saver when students are so lost they cannot clearly identify their writing needs, and the information allows tutors to prioritize weaknesses and construct effective tutorials. As tutors work with students, the scoring guides can become a form of feedback for the faculty. Similarly, writing center interactions via referral sheets can show faculty effective strategies for dealing with typical problems students encounter when composing discourse and for revising assignments for future use. Instructors get a clear idea of how the writing center can help students focus ideas for clarity, master the rules of mechanics and punctuation, and develop cohesive strategies for editing grammar and format. As faculty collaborate with the writing center, they can learn strategies for curbing unintentional plagiarism. Through the writing center, students can develop their abilities to glean ideas from research and to express them in their own language rather than plagiarizing.

The following scoring guide was developed by our writing center and the Department of Criminal Justice after instructors discovered that students were composing papers the night before at a community college in the Midwest where I was Coordinator of Developmental Programs. The guide was based on an assignment in which students read a law-enforcement novel from an approved reading list (the majority of the choices were novels by Joseph Wambaugh). The students then prepared a review in terms of an author's key ideas toward law enforcement, the book's relevance to classroom discussions, and the practicality of the book for those who work in a specific branch of law enforcement (e.g., a community police department, the FBI, etc.). On the guide that follows, the 3 and 4 scores include the following: an evaluation of the rhetorical richness of the draft, an evaluation of organization and development, and an indicator of problems in language and usage. The 1 and 2 scores are abbreviated since organization and language issues are moot if students have not met the appropriate goals for the assignment. We included a statement in category 2 addressing those who submitted significant numbers of errors in otherwise competent papers.

Scoring Guide

Book Review for Introduction to Criminal Justice

4   The paper shows signs of very good progress toward meeting the goals of the assignment. It is in the form of a book review geared toward an audience of people working for a specific police agency. The essay contains a good introduction to the topic and one that appeals to the specific audience. The introduction concludes with a clear thesis that effectively focuses the key assertions you wish to make concerning the book. Each of your paragraphs is well organized. Each starts with a clear topic sentence and is followed by well-focused supporting points adequately illustrated by good examples and details. Paragraphs effectively synthesize the main points the book presents and evaluate them for their usefulness and practicality for police work. You have done a good job in connecting the ideas in each paragraph to your central thesis. While the paper is satisfactory, it still needs work in organization and development. Grammar and spelling errors exist, but they are not serious enough to distract the reader from the ideas you wish to communicate.

3   The paper is satisfactory, but it lacks the quality of a score of 4 in one or more ways. While your essay is in a form of a review, it does not go into the depth necessary to make it

impressive. You need to revise your paper for a clearer thesis and more effective organization. While you make a number of good assertions, they tend to be superficial; you need to generate more assertions and/or develop them with clear examples and illustrations. You also need to make better connections between your paragraph assertions and your central thesis. You have also made a number of sentence-level errors (fragments, run-ons, impacted and/or derailed sentences). You tend to lack connections between sentences and/or paragraphs. Your paper contains some word-level grammar and/or spelling errors. To improve the paper, you should schedule an appointment with the Writing Center and/or your instructor to discuss the areas you can improve.

2   The paper is not in the form of a book review. Rather, the paper retells the story in chronological order. While the paper may be well organized, it does not do what the assignment asks you to do—identify the book's major assertions about police work, show how they compare with the concepts you have learned in class, and evaluate them as to their practicality and usefulness for an officer in a specific law-enforcement agency. If this were a final draft, the paper contains too many sentence-level structural errors, word-level grammatical errors and/or spelling mistakes to allow the paper to receive a satisfactory grade. You are to see the instructor and make an appointment with the Writing Center within the next two class days. You then will have a week to revise the draft and schedule another conference with the instructor and the Writing Center. These steps must be done before submitting the next formal draft. See your syllabus for the next submission date.

1   The paper is unacceptable because it does not complete the requirements of the assignment. The paper lacks focus, organization, and development. The paper also shows that you lack an essential grasp of the ideas presented in the novel. You are to see the instructor and make an appointment with the Writing Center within the next two class days. You will need to spend a significant amount of time with both tutors. Be prepared to discuss the book with a reading tutor and to compose a new draft with the help of the writing tutor. Both tutors will provide you with progress reports that you must attach to the next draft. See your syllabus for the next submission date.

Only the top two scores address specific rhetorical and grammatical features because the papers basically address the tasks that the assignment requires. The bottom two scores indicate papers that are basically off-topic. Since papers receiving a 1 or a 2 needed to be rewritten, the scores did not address specific considerations other than the warning statement about editing in the 2 score.

Because a significant number of the students enrolled in Introduction to Criminal Justice were also taking a developmental writing course, we decided that each student should write four drafts, each one due at two-week intervals. The instructor used the scoring guide to evaluate each draft by highlighting those significant points applicable to a student's paper and an overall score. Besides indicating specific improvements that students needed to make, the highlighted features also provided good referral information for writing center tutors. For example, while a number of papers received an overall rating of 3 on the third draft, faculty also highlighted the following statement from the 2 score indicating that students needed to address structural issues: "If this were a final draft, the paper contains too many sentence-level structural errors, word-level grammatical errors and/or spelling mistakes to allow the paper to receive a satisfactory grade." Because structural error was a significant problem, the writing center staff created a number of group tutorials that instructors required students to attend.

Below is a sample of the work presented by a student enrolled in a developmental composition class along with Introduction to Criminal Justice. The first draft received an overall score of 1; the second, a 2; the third, a 3, and the fourth (the final paper), an A, which testifies to the success of the scoring guide.

Draft 1   Score: **1**

The New Centurions

Three men in the police academy, all coming for different reasons, all from different backgrounds. Serge Duncan who is an ex-Marine and is trying desperately to find his identity both as an officer and as a Chicano. Gus Plebesly had a great attraction for prostitutes, but still is not sure of if he makes the grade as a man and a cop. Roy Fehler is a very refined individual, who finds he has a prejudice against blacks. Each with his own problem and each with their own cure.

The New Centurions is a griping tale of what it really is like to be a police officer straight from the mind of Joseph Wambaugh. While others tell you the story, Wambaugh makes you feel as if you are there. In all of his stories Wambaugh has the exact science of policework in little areas that you don't even realize is the true story. California and especially Hollenbeck division seems to be Wambaughs greatest setting. From the gratuities to the facts of what early police stations were hiring for personnel, everything that we are learning, is in this book. The best experience is the beat itself because how can any person actually know what he is going to do without practice. The books teach the individual how to do the things but people are unpredictable and will do what they are used to.

Draft 2   Score: **2**

The New Centurions

In modern American society, crime increases each year at a rapid rate. The police and society itself to change at a rate equal to or faster than the crime. With the crime police have more stress on them than ever before. Not only to catch the criminals but also to conform and work as a team. At the same time having individual stress and having to deal with it alone.

In Joseph Wambaugh's *The New Centurions* he brings out this point that police not only have stress from the job but also problems and stress from home. He goes right to the heart of the problem by dipping into the thoughts and the feelings of three policemen fresh out of the academy and follows them through their first five years on the force. The first Serge, or Sergio, Duran who is an ex-Marine and is trying to find his identity as a Chicano in a white oriented department that hasn't accepted him as an officer yet. Second, Gus Flebesly, who is trying to convince himself that he measures up as a man and an officer. The girls are attracted to him, yet due to his size he tries to convince himself that he could do the job if force were necessary in a conflict situation. Last, Roy Fehler, who thought of himself as a very refined individual, and finds he has a prejudice against blacks, while working in an all black neighborhood.

The conflict these men felt are the same conflicts that officers feel still today. Unfortunately their cures are the same also. When men have doubts, as these men did, in themselves others start doubting them.

They look for a crutch to rely on most of the time, it is alcohol. As the men's self-esteem falls apart so do their performances and their relationships, as in Roy's case in the book. By the time he discovered who his real friend were, the men form his training, he didn't have time to enjoy it. I believe this is basically the major point that Wambaugh was trying to get across. Wambaugh tells little stories in each of his novels in each chapter. He inspires us to think while we read and extract the stories that we can use on the job and everyday.

I enjoyed the book and the way Wambaugh slipped his little stories in the ends of the chapters in the book. You think you are just reading some insignificant detail when in reality it is probably the most important part of the novel.

There are only a few things that disappointed me in the book. One was how he used Spanish and didn't give us what was being said. Next, how he used police lingo, but the reason for this is the audience he was trying to reach was the police.

Overall I would give this book an S. Due to hard reading if your not equipped with the necessary tools for reading this book.

Draft 3   Score: **3**

The New Centurions

In modern American society, crime increases each year at a rapid rate. The police and society itself has to change at a rate equal to or faster than the crime. With the crime police have more stress on them than before. Not only to catch the criminals but also to conform and work as a team. At the same time having individual stress and having to deal it alone.

In Joseph Wambaugh's *The New Centurions* he brings out this point that police not only have stress from the job but also problems and stress from home. He goes right to the heart of the problem by dipping into the thoughts and feelings of three policemen fresh out of the academy and follows them through their first five years on the force. The first Serge, or Sergio, duran who is an ex-Marine and is trying to find his identity as a Chicano in a white oriented department that hasn't accepted him as an officer yet. Second, Gus Plebesly, who is trying to convince himself that he measures up as a man and an officer. The girls are attracted to him, but due to his size he tries to convince himself that he could do the job if force were necessary in a conflict situation. Last, Roy Fehler, who thought of himself as a very refined individual, and finds he has a prejudice against blacks, while working in an all black neighborhood.

The conflicts these men felt are the same conflicts that officers feel still today. Unfortunately their cures are the same also. When men have doubts, as these men did, in themselves others start doubting them. They look for a crutch to rely on most of the time it is alcohol. As the men's self-esteem falls apart so do them and their relationships, as in Roy's case in the story. By the time he knew what he wanted and could deal with it, he was dead and had no chance at his happiness. Like most officers he didn't have many friends when he found some in his fellow officers he died. Wambaugh tells little stories in each of his novels in each chapter. He inspires us to think while we read and extract the stories that we can use everyday.

I enjoyed the book and the way Wambaugh slipped his little stories in the ends of Chapters. You think it is just ending the chapter and that there is no significant ideas in that part. When in reality it gives us a bigger tale than the story itself.

There are only a few things that I didn't like about the book. One was how put some spanish words in and didn't give you the meanings of them. Second, was the way he used police lingo, but I believe that he thought that his audience was going to be mostly police. And lastly, I didn't like the way he put the setting in California and used the names of cities and places we wouldn't know unless we lived there.

Draft 4   Grade: **A**

The New Centurions

In modern American society, crime increases each year at a very rapid rate. This causes the police and societies roles in law enforcement to change at a rate equal to or faster than the crimes rate of increase. With the crime, police have more stress on them than ever before. Not only to catch the criminals but also to, after being thrown into an unfamiliar situation, conform and work as a team with people that they may not like. At home they have to deal with the stress of everyday life and act is if there is nothing wrong with them, not letting out their feelings because they have no one to talk to about the job unless they have police friends. Rookies however, don't have police friends most of the time, at least ones they can talk to without being laughed at, to help them make this big transition from their beliefs to the departments. This causes self doubt and more stress for young officers and eventually burnout as their career progresses.

In Joseph Wambaugh's *The New Centurions* he brings out this point that police not only have stress from the job but also problems and stress from home and no way of dealing with either form. He goes right to the heart of the problem by dipping into the thoughts and the feelings of three policemen fresh out of the academy and follows them through their first five years on the force. The first Serge, or Sergio Duran who is an ex-Marine and is trying to find his identity as a Chicano in a white orientated department that hasn't accepted him as an officer yet. Second, Gus Plebesly, who is trying to convince himself that he measures up as a man and an officer. The girls are attracted to him, yet due to his size he tries to convince himself that he could do the job if force were necessary in a conflict situation. Last, Roy Fehler, who thought of himself as a very refined individual, and finds he has a prejudice against blacks, while working in an all black neighborhood.

The conflict these men felt are the same conflicts that officers feel still today. Unfortunately their cures are the same also. When men have doubts, as these men did, in themselves others start doubting them also. They look for a crutch to rely on, most of the time it is alcohol. As the men's self-esteem falls apart so do their performances and their relationships, as in Roy's case in the book. By the time he discovered who his real friends were, the men from his training school, he didn't have time to enjoy it. This is basically the major point that Wambaugh is trying to get across. While your alive, live your life, don't worry it away.

Wambaugh tells little stories in each of his novels in each chapter. He inspires us to think while we read and extract the stories that we can use on the job and everyday. I enjoyed the book and the way he put those little stories in the book. You think you are just reading some insignificant detail when in reality it is probably the most important part of the novel.

There are only a few things that disappointed me in the book. One was how he used Spanish and didn't give us what was being said. Next, how he used police lingo and left a person that isn't on the job wondering what he was talking about, but the reason for this is the audience he was trying to reach was the police.

Because the score on the first draft indicated that the student did not understand the novel, both the student and the tutor spent a great deal of time discussing the meaning of the novel and discovering key assertions that the Wambaugh made concerning police work. The second draft was an improvement over the first, but the student essentially retold the story.

Consequently, during the next two weeks, the student worked on organizing and developing his ideas. The score of 3 from the third draft indicated that he was on target but still needed to develop ideas more. The guide also indicated that he needed to address serious problems in structure. Because the guide served as a referral form, the student attended almost all of the grammar tutorials offered at the writing center. Because this student was willing to invest a great deal of time and energy in each draft, he improved dramatically. His final grade of "A" was testimony to the success of the scoring guide as a clear source of feedback for students and writing center staff.

Faculty were quite pleased with the holistic scoring guide. One provided the following testimonial:

> While evaluating rough drafts has not solved all of the student problems in writing, students have nonetheless benefited from this approach because they have learned better writing skills. I need to take only a minute or two to skim over a draft and to highlight its strengths and weaknesses on the holistic scoring guide.
>
> Writing scoring guides also force me to evaluate the assignments that I give. In the process of creating a scoring guide, I must judge for myself what constitutes a superior draft as opposed to an average one. I must also think about those pitfalls that students will fall into, and I am able to guide these students better as they go about writing the paper. Whereas I never thought about process before, I now think about the strategies students must master before they are able to compose an acceptable draft. The holistic guide also helps me to be more consistent as I grade final drafts of a given assignment.
>
> I am pleased with the final papers that I now evaluate. I know that students are not writing the papers the night before. I am able to anticipate problems as I write assignments, and the process helps me to be more organized. I am able to give students solid criticism and strategies for improving their work rather than merely telling them that their writing is unsatisfactory and leaving it up to the students to figure out what is wrong. Most of all, I now realize that good writing is more than teaching grammar and punctuation.

The scoring guide has helped instructors create more meaningful writing assignments and has produced better writing from students. Because the Criminal Justice faculty members noted that the quality of papers improved drastically from the year before, they implemented similar scoring methods with other classes.

Students likewise seem to appreciate holistic scoring. Several students were willing to write testimonials. A typical one states,

> Holistic scoring is a totally new concept to me. I find that tells me exactly what an "A" paper should look like. I don't have to guess or "psych out" the teacher as I had to do in the past. In the past I had a very hard time determining what the teacher wanted when she would make comments on my paper.
>
> When I get back a draft that has been scored, I know exactly what I must do to improve my paper, but I know how much improvement that I must make. If the teacher highlights something in a lower score range, I know that the designated problems on my draft are serious. If I receive a higher score on another aspect of my draft, I know that I am basically in the ballpark even though I must make improvements. I always have an idea of the seriousness of any problems on my draft.

While many students initially balked at the idea of writing multiple drafts with feedback from a scoring guide, they came to appreciate the specific ideas for revision the scoring guide provided them. The majority of the students in the course felt their writing skills improved. Many went so far as to claim that they would seek out another faculty member who used this scoring method since they saw this type of holistic scoring as objective. Writing center staff felt that the guide allowed for clear lines of communication with course instructors.

The use of a scoring guide created from a blend of holistic, analytic, and primary trait scoring for responding to student writing has received a favorable response. Students as well as faculty feel that scoring guides have eliminated the ambiguity that sometimes accompanies writing assignments because holistic scoring presents a clear definition of what constitutes a good paper. While this method for feedback cannot possibly address all writing problems, it has revitalized instructors' interests in developing writing assignments for their classes and has increased the value of the writing center as a place of service for everyone

References

Bauer, B.A. (1981). A study of the reliabilities and the cost-effectiveness of three methods of assessment for writing ability. (ERIC Document no. 216 357).

Dawe, A., et. al. (1990). Assessing English skills: Writing. A resource book for adult basic education. (ERIC document no. 241 956).

Diederich, P. (1974). *Measuring growth in English*. Urbana, IL: NCTE.

Faigley, L., Cherry, R.D., Jolliffe, D.A., & Skinner, A.M. (1985). *Assessing writers'knowledge and processes of composing*. Norwood, NJ: Ablex.

Freedman, S.W. (1981). Influences on evaluators of expository essays: Beyond the text. *Research in the Teaching of English, 15*, 245-255.

Huot, B. (1990). The literature of direct writing assessment: Major concerns and prevailing trends. *Review of Educational Research, 60*, 237-263.

Lloyd-Jones, R. (1977). Primary trait scoring. In C. Cooper & L. Odell (Eds.), *Evaluating writing*. (pp. 33-48) Urbana, IL: NCTE.

Paulis, C. (1985, October). Holistic scoring: A revision strategy. *Clearing House, 59*, 57-60.

Westcott, W. & Gardner, P. (1984, December). Holistic scoring as a teaching device. *Teaching English in the Two-Year College, 11*, 35-39.

White, E. (1985). *Teaching and assessing writing*. San Francisco: Jossey-Bass.

Centering:
What Writing Centers Need to Do

Joseph Saling
Massachusetts Bay Community College

Introduction

Writing centers should be at the center of the debate over educational reform, yet most of us in the writing center profession still feel marginalized. If we are to move to the center, we need to look at our own practices first and change those that keep us out of the debate.

Two Stories

Last spring, I attended a meeting at the University of Massachusetts, Amherst, to learn more about a joint admissions program that guarantees students a place at the university after they complete their first two years at a community college. As part of the presentations that day, four students, who were among the first to come into the university under the joint admissions plan, discussed their experiences. All four praised the program and said they would not be at school if they had not had the opportunity to go to a community college first and had not had the guidance from both the community college and the university that the program provides. Each also said, though, that their first semesters at the university were a nightmare. Their GPAs dropped. They felt lost in the immense size of the university, and they were not prepared for how different classes would be: lecture halls filled with 200 students, professors who were virtually inaccessible, and grades determined on the basis of just two tests.

In the question-and-answer period, they were asked what community colleges and the university could do to make the transition easier for future students. Most of us expected to hear things like more counseling at the community college level or more support services at the university. Instead, we were told to put students at the community colleges in touch with students who had already transferred to the university. In fact, one of the students, Michael Lombard from Bristol Community College, said he and another student from Bristol had begun a sort of underground railroad, bringing students from Bristol to the campus, letting them stay in their dorm rooms, talking to them about the kinds of services and activities that were there, and taking them to classes to let them see what they could expect when they arrived.

This collaborative approach to helping other students make a difficult transition should not surprise anyone who works in a writing center. We've long known the value of students working together to solve common problems. We've seen first hand that, when peers interact, they learn from one another.

Here's another story. A couple of years ago, Kelly Cook-McEachern and I took a group of students to the National Peer Tutoring Conference in Vermont. These were not tutors. Only one had ever been paid for tutoring, and that had been for his work as a mentor tutor in the learning disabilities program. These were members of a group at Massachusetts Bay Community College known as Core Writers, a loosely organized group of students, faculty, and staff whose only requirement for membership is that they consider themselves writers and demonstrate that fact either by writing for one of the Writing Lab's publications or by making themselves available on a totally voluntary basis to talk to other writers who come to the Lab.

Linda, who had become a Core Writer while she was still in pre-freshman level basic writing, told what it was like to talk to other students about their writing and how she had learned to think of herself as a writer in the process. When she was challenged during the question-and-answer period by a tutor in the audience who wondered how she could help other students without having any kind of formal training, she gave an elegant and theoretically correct defense of the benefits of collaborative learning. Takeshi, a student from Japan who had originally come to the Lab for help with vocabulary and grammar, talked about how writing movie reviews and "think" pieces on the arts for the Lab's bi-weekly publication had changed his image of himself. "I never in my dreams," he said, "thought of standing here and calling myself a writer. But as long as they let me write, I will be one."

Another student, Leo, who had a learning disability so severe that some of his high school teachers had indicated on his records that they considered him to be unteachable, chose the sessions he went to carefully so he would have something to bring back and help improve the way our own lab operates. Sunday afternoon before we left campus, Leo said the weekend had helped him decide what he wanted to do with his life. He wanted to be, he said, a college teacher.

Again, people who work in writing labs should not be surprised at how well these students represented themselves and the school. Students become engaged in learning and helping others learn when they believe the work they are doing is important and when their individual efforts are supported by more knowledgeable people who belong to a community the students feel is worth belonging to.

Our Current State of the Profession

Eleven years ago, Stephen North published in *College English* what has become the declaration of independence for writing centers. "The Idea of a Writing Center" set us free to explore learning in new ways. We no longer had to construct apologies for what we do. We were not part of any curriculum, and we were engaged in a marvelous Socratic experiment in which writers, and by extension learners, talk to one another about what they are doing.

In the decade that has followed, we've discovered a great deal about the way people learn. We know first hand, for example, what theorists such as Friere and Shor mean when they say learning needs to be contextualized in ways that are meaningful for the learner.[1] We've witnessed, as John Dewey did, the value of real work in helping students acquire knowledge. And we've practiced in our own centers what the linguist James Paul Gee has called "scaffolding" by providing support for people attempting to acquire a new discourse. Peer tutoring, collaborative learning, and collaborative writing are all part of our special domain, and, if we haven't written the book on these topics, we should.

We've also grown in stature as a profession. Dissertations focused on writing centers are now a regular occurrence. We have two respected national journals and now a national conference. Most colleges and universities and many high schools have writing centers, some even directed by tenured faculty.

Yet, in many ways, we haven't grown at all. Eric Hobson has observed,

> Often Writing Center Professionals are the only people at their institutions to understand what writing centers do and what writing centers mean; there is a great deal of isolation—physical and intellectual—experienced in this community. (7)

Dave Healy adds,

> People who work in writing centers often fall prey to professional insecurity. We feel misunderstood and unappreciated in our own departments ... and in the larger academy. Our marginal status makes us feel exploited by those with more institutional power and vulnerable in times of retrenchment. (16)

We know we are engaged in essential activities. *We* know we have a lot to add to the current dialogue about educational reform and that we should be at the center of the debate. Yet, instead of making our voices heard where they need to be heard, many of us spend a great deal of time worrying from one day to the next whether our jobs will be there next term.

It would be easy to point a finger at our professional colleagues and at the institutions that house us and blame them for shortsightedness, for rigid adherence to outdated concepts of learning, for jealously guarding an exclusionary authoritarian structure that impedes rather than facilitates real learning. But, before we do, we need to examine our own practices and ask ourselves why, after all this time and all this learning, we are still on the margin.

Looking at Ourselves

In reviewing *The Writing Center: New Directions*, Jeanette Harris lists several characteristics that identify our profession as it enters its second generation. "First," she says, "we are primarily pragmatics rather than theorists," more concerned with "what works and what doesn't" than with theoretical considerations. The second trait is that "we are storytellers first and scholars second" and "are most comfortable when we are telling other writing center people what we did." The third is that "we are a well-defined discourse community ... an almost intimate profession whose members know the same people and read the same texts." Harris ends her review by concluding, "We haven't changed all that much: the second generation of writing centers is much like the first .... If there are differences ... they are superficial rather than integral" (209).

Given the nature of our work, these traits are understandable. Because we work with students one-on-one or in small groups, we need to be more concerned with particulars than with generalizations, and the nature of our work, which is primarily talk, lends itself to story telling. People in our profession are well read and make a conscious effort (as evidenced by the vitality of the WCenter list on Internet) to stay abreast of what others are doing. And the fact that we are slow to change isn't bad if what we do works for the students we are there for.

Evidence of a Need for Action

But there is evidence that things aren't working as well as they should. After four years of studying, Leo, the student who wanted to teach college, is still at Mass Bay. He's twenty-eight, and he's taking two courses a semester. He's basically given up on the idea of being a professor and is happy about the job he recently acquired—sweeping floors behind the meat counter in a food co-op. Linda, who gave such a brilliant defense of collaborative learning, dropped out of school the semester after she so clearly demonstrated her understanding of both the value and the process of learning. Both these students and countless others we see, students who come alive in the center, need more than we can offer them in the limited contact we have with them.

And it's not just the "at-risk students" who can benefit by what we know. We've seen it over and over. The students who become engaged in the process of their own education and who have the opportunity to stay engaged, the students who become active participants in the dialogue about knowledge and who can stay a part of that dialogue, do better and go farther than those who are excluded.

Our Responsibility

Too much of our educational structure excludes students. Nancy Grimm recently observed that "in a writing center, one discovers how smart students are and how arbitrary and limiting linguistic conventions and educational hierarchies can be" (5). Since we see the truth of these observations first hand, we have an obligation to both the institution and the students enrolled there to share what we know. And if what we do makes a difference in students' lives, then we have an obligation as a profession to put ourselves in the center of educational reform.

How to Move Ourselves to the Center

Before we can put ourselves there, though, we need to change some of our own practices that keep us from the center. Three things come to mind. First, we have to become less timid about theory and more aggressive about articulating not only the reasons behind things we do but also the philosophy that informs those reasons. Then we have to expand the scope of our programs to make them more inclusive and more an integral part of the educational process. And finally, we have to examine what seems to be conventional wisdom in the writing center to avoid slipping into a restrictive and restraining orthodoxy.

Becoming Less Timid About Theory

If we expect what we do to make any real difference in the lives of more than just a few students, we have to become aware of why what we do works and then share that awareness with the larger educational community. We have to be what we hope the students we work with become—good rhetoricians who not only understand the subject matter but also understand the audience we are presenting to. What that audience wants is two things: (1) proof of the effectiveness of what we do and (2) explanations of why what we do works. I don't mean we should become less pragmatic; we still need to know what works. But, if we can demonstrate to others that what we do works and then tell them why it works, we will have taken a giant step toward making the academy a less hostile environment for the majority of students.

At Massachusetts Bay Community College, we have been working to articulate a theory of necessary communities. Briefly, a necessary community is nothing other than a community that forms to fill a particular need, and the communities we are talking about are learning communities that engage faculty and students in meaningful work because, we believe, students don't really learn until they are engaged in work that is meaningful to them.

We are also rethinking the model for learning by looking at models from other areas, such as the model for change from neurolinguistic programming. That model identifies five logical levels that affect how people perform: environment, behaviors, capabilities, beliefs and values, and identity (Dilts 1). Writing center people know almost intuitively the necessity of addressing each of these levels as they help students identify themselves as writers. As our program at Mass Bay evolves, we are making a conscious effort to understand how our sense of necessary communities addresses each of those levels.

Our current theory and philosophy are embedded in our mission statement, which is now a part of all Writing Lab publications. We also have made it a priority among the staff to write articles for both internal and external publications that focus on how the theory that has evolved from writing center practice can be applied to other areas of education. We make a conscious effort to demonstrate the effectiveness of a practice based on that theory by keeping meticulous records that document our effectiveness: we solicit feedback from the students; we know not only how many we see, but also what percentage of the student population they represent; and we also know how students who use the lab perform on the writing assessment test that is given to all students at the school. And we make it a point to be a part of every committee that looks at curriculum. Our efforts at doing so have resulted in several collaborative arrangements with teachers who want to reform the way people are taught.

At the same time, we are constantly examining our mission statement and our sense of the theory that informs it and making a conscious effort to model the process of change by letting theory inform our practice while we let practice evolve theory.

Expanding the Scope of our Programs

If we really want to talk to our colleagues about educational reform, about the value of building learning communities, and about opening their classrooms to real student involvement, we need to demonstrate that our ideas work not for just a select group of hand-picked people, but for all the students who come into our centers. We need to model the openness we want other teachers to adopt. Unfortunately, many of the communities we've created keep us from doing those things.

"When I hear the word *tutor*," Dina Fayer, a peer tutor at the University of California–Berkeley wrote in *Writing Lab Newsletter*, "I think of authorities who teach other individuals better proficiency in their area of expertise." In her article that illustrated how she needed to break some of the established rules about the way peer tutors relate to their clients, she went on to say that the word *peer* made her think of her own friends and their relationships, "which are based on humor, parties, gossip, and fellow-feeling." When she put the terms *peer* and *tutor* together, she concluded, "I can't think of two concepts more irreconcilable" (13). Yet peer tutoring is what we do.

At Mass Bay, we realized that as long as we talk about the students we see as "THEM" and about the Writing Lab staff as "US," there really wasn't much difference between the Lab experience and the experience a student has conferencing with his or her teacher. As Dave Healy has noted, "Unless the writing center provides an alternative to the classroom, unless writers experience something there that is qualitatively different from what they find elsewhere on their journey through the curriculum, then justifying the center's existence seems problematic" (27). If we can't justify our own existence, we certainly can't center ourselves in the debate about educational reform. Consequently, we deliberately set out to make the Lab a different kind of place, a place where the only differences between staff and students would be that staff are paid to be there during certain hours and that staff have a continuing responsibility to create new opportunities for all members of the community to explore the use of language.

We had an advantage at Mass Bay that a lot of writing centers don't have. We had two credit-bearing courses on the books that were a requirement for approximately 35% of all incoming students. Those two courses enroll close to a thousand students a year, which gave us a captive audience. We took advantage of that audience to create Core Writers. We made buttons and gave them out to people and said the buttons meant they were willing to talk to other people about writing. We wore the buttons, too, and told the students the only difference between them and us was that, if they saw someone coming they didn't want to talk to, they could take the button off; we couldn't.

Next we began exploring ways to give students a real voice in the college community. We started with a bi-weekly publication that included writing not just from students but from faculty and staff, and we openly solicited submissions from the entire campus. In the beginning, *CORE NEWS* was three pages. It quickly grew to a twenty-page digest format.

We didn't stop there. We opened the possibility of students' giving workshops on topics of their choice. We created a forum for students and faculty to present works in progress. Core Writers organized and sponsored a poetry rally that has turned into an annual event that attracts professional poets from all over the country who come to the school to read their work alongside students and staff. This year, we've initiated an international salon, a weekly program at which students and faculty meet to learn about and discuss other cultures. In response to student requests, we have started ESL conversation groups and reading and writing workshops in which students select the material to be read and discussed.

An important part of our efforts is to give the students a legitimate voice on campus so that the use of language in the institution becomes important to them. Our weekly Lab meetings have always been open to anyone who wants to attend, and we make a concerted effort to get students involved in other activities normally reserved for faculty and administrators. For example, we have arranged for students to partici- pate in the norming and scoring process for the writing division's exit assessment, and this year we have increased our efforts to get students included on committees students don't normally participate in, espe- cially those committees concerned with curriculum and institutional planning.

All of this activity does not mean we still do not work with students one-on-one with their classroom assignments. Nor does the idea of making students our peers mean we have given up being experts when it comes to the way language is used in the academy. What it does mean is that students are much more willing to assume the responsibility of talking to one another about their work and that their efforts and enthu- siasm for things academic are more visible to the rest of the college community.

Avoiding Orthodoxy

Finally, avoiding orthodoxy means we remain a creative and vital force within our own communities and in the larger educational commu- nity. It means we find new ways to enhance student learning and engagement in that learning. Last year, a group of students at Mass Bay came to me and proposed that the Lab offer a three-credit sophomore level course in creative writing. Conventional wisdom says that writing centers should not be offering credit-bearing courses because that in- volves us in the process of evaluation. What we did was allow the students to design the course and then worked with them to make them responsible for their own evaluation. The result is a course in which students negotiate contracts with lab facilitators for the amount of work they will do to receive a particular grade and then work with one another in small group workshops to explore all kinds of creative writing activi- ties.

Our effort to avoid orthodoxy is at the heart of our weekly staff meetings and is the primary motivational force that keeps all of us making entries on a dialogue journal we keep on the computer in the Writing Lab.

Out of those meetings and from that journal have come the seeds for such programs as Core Writers (when we began questioning the idea of training tutors and then calling what the tutors and students did "collaborative learning"), a communally written novel (when we simply asked ourselves whether students could learn at least as much from a collaborative writing project as they did from individual writing assignments), *CORE NEWS* and the Poetry Rally (when we saw how much more enthusiastically members of the learning community in the Lab worked on projects that were meaningful to them than when they worked on artificial assignments made in the classroom).

We have a real fear of becoming complacent, of settling into an orthodoxy that may be comfortable but that can also be deadly to the excitement we feel and limit the possibility of what we can learn. The greatest threat from orthodoxy, though, is that it can make us forget that the key to student-centered education is full participation by the student in all aspects of his or her education. When our policies exclude students, either by regimenting what they do when they come to the center or by limiting their access to the opportunities the center offers, we have become as rigid as the rest of the academy. Then it won't matter whether we are at the center of the discussion about educational reform because we won't really have anything new to offer.

Notes

[1]See, for example, Ira Shor's "Monday Morning Fever: Critical Literacy and the Generative Theme of 'Work'" in *Freire for the Classroom*.

Works Cited

Dewey, John. *The School and Society and The Child and the Curriculum*. Chicago: U of Chicago P, 1990.

Dilts, Robert. *Changing Belief Systems With NLP*. Cupertino: Meta, 1990.

Fayer, Dina. "Tutors' Column: Orthodoxy and Effectiveness." *Writing Lab Newsletter* 18.5 (1994): 13.

Gee, James Paul. "Literacy, Discourse, and Linguistics: Introduction." *Journal of Education* 17.1 (1989): 5-25.

Grimm, Nancy. "Contesting 'The Idea of a Writing Center': The Politics of Writing Center Research." *Writing Lab Newsletter* 17.1 (1992): 5-6.

Harris, Jeanette. Rev. of *The Writing Center: New Directions*. *The Writing Center Journal* 12 (1992): 203-10.

Healy, Dave. "A Defense of Dualism: The Writing Center and the Classroom." *The Writing Center Journal* 14.1 (1993): 16-29.

Hobson, Eric. "Coming Out of the Silence." *Writing Lab Newsletter* 17.6 (1993): 7-8.

North, Stephen M. "The Idea of a Writing Center." *College English* 46 (1984): 433-46.

Shor, Ira, ed. *Freire for the Classroom: A Sourcebook for Liberatory Teaching*. Portsmouth: Boynton/Cook, 1987.

Accreditation and the Writing Center: A Proposal for Action

Joe Law
Texas Christian University

A writing center's funding depends upon how its effectiveness is perceived; likewise, writing center staff wanting increased recognition as professionals gain that respect according to the way they are perceived. Clearly, then, evaluating and presenting oneself and one's program are crucial activities. Unfortunately, many writing centers are still perceived as ancillary to "real" instruction and the writing center staff regarded as second- or third-class members of the academy.

At stake here is not merely the bruising of an individual ego or a petty academic version of sibling rivalry. The way others—especially administrators—see the writing center is directly connected with our prospering—indeed, with our surviving. Everyone has heard horror stories of budget cuts and closings facing writing centers across the country; you may even know them at first hand. Let me take only one of many possible examples to illustrate: on March 17, 1993, the WCenter network contained an urgent message requesting national support for the writing center at California State–Chico, which is widely considered a model program. The program at Cal State–Chico has not been canceled as it looked as if it was going to be; however, the center was granted three years to find an independent source of funding if it is to continue.

It is in such a context that the present proposal ought to be seen. I would like to suggest establishing a national accrediting agency to evaluate individual writing centers and "certify" that they meet a nationally recognized standard at one of several specific levels. This agency would be roughly analogous to such established agencies as the Southern Association of Colleges and Schools (SACS). SACS is a regional organization covering schools in eleven states, but the other regional organizations operate in the same way and with nearly identical procedures. Thus, whenever I mention SACS, I mean those other regional accrediting agencies as well. Ideally, membership in the writing center accrediting agency would confer a status analogous to accreditation by SACS or its regional equivalent.

Although I'll discuss some possible configurations for this agency and suggest ways in which it might be implemented, the plan advanced here is necessarily sketchy; in fact, the holes in it are big enough to drive an eighteen-wheeler through. Nonetheless, such a plan is both feasible and beneficial and ought to be pursued.

If accreditation is to have any validity, it must come from an agency that is national in scope and recognized as a legitimate professional entity. At the moment, only one group dedicated exclusively to writing center concerns fits that description—the National Writing Centers Association. NWCA coordinates regional organizations and provides a national directory of writing centers. And it already has a fairly high professional profile nationally. It sponsors two journals and an annual national conference, bestows scholarships and professional awards, and provides guidance for establishing new writing centers. Because the NWCA is dedicated to writing center concerns, it would seem a more appropriate group to determine writing center standards than the College Reading and Learning Association, the agency through which Bonnie Devet has suggested writing center certification.

The NWCA's level of activity means that its various committees are already very busy; clearly, reviewing certification applications and visiting sites will require a substantial number of additional people. The certification teams could consist of writing center directors from across the country who apply for those position. Once their credentials are approved by an NWCA committee, these people could serve a limited term, perhaps three or five years, during which they would divide applications and site visits among themselves. At least initially, the teams visiting a center should consist of two or at most three members.

These visits would be carried out in the same way as SACS visits currently are. Before the site visit by the accrediting team, the local center would have gone through a two-phase self-evaluation, consisting of both an internal evaluation by the staff of the center and an outside evaluation by other members of the college or university community. The reports of both groups would be submitted to the NWCA team before it arrives on campus.

That much of the plan is reasonably easy. The difficulties start when we ask a simple but really specific question: just what should be evaluated by the local groups and the NWCA team? At least for starters, we should follow the SACS model. The center being evaluated should begin with an explicit statement of specific goals and objectives, followed by its plan for reaching those goals. The discussion that would ensue from formulating and evaluating these two items is crucial, for it should help to address a long-standing problem in writing center work—how do we evaluate what we do? I am not optimistic enough—or naive enough—to believe that this approach solves the problem, but it should be much easier to quantify and document how well we meet precisely specified objectives than to treat anecdotal material or impressionistic reactions as evidence of our success levels. If, to take a simplistic example, we want to teach students to write a formulaic essay that will pass a state-mandated exit exam, we can certainly document how many of the previously failing students that we work with eventually pass that exam and at what point. Meeting more complex goals would be more difficult to determine, but looking for the verifiable components of those goals should help us to evaluate our work more effectively.

Answers will be clearer in evaluating the staff of the writing center. That should begin with the director. Is the director a full-time professional member of the university? Does he or she have faculty or equivalent administrative rank? Does the director have graduate training, publications, or extensive experience in writing center administration, composition, and/or rhetoric? Does he or she evidence continued professional growth and activity specifically in the writing center field? If the director has a faculty appointment in an English department, will writing center work and publications be valued in tenure decisions or is the director expected to publish in a literary specialty?

If the center employs professional full-time or part-time staff in addition to a director, similar questions ought to be asked of them. If the center is operated by students, issues of on-site training should be examined. Some schools offer credit-bearing, semester-length courses for their tutors, and such approaches would certainly be preferable to less systematic, briefer ones. Separate but related criteria would need to be established for graduate students and undergraduate peer tutors.

Another area that should be assessed prior to the certification team's visit is the extent to which equipment and physical facilities assist the writing center in realizing its goals. Again, many of the items will be obvious. In addition to such readily evident concerns as the quantity, age, and condition of computer equipment, the degree to which that equipment is being used to its full potential should also be examined. If, for example, computers are networked across campus, is that technology being used to enhance the writing center's operation? Or are computers used only for drills? Likewise, criteria for assessing the adequacy of physical resources should be established.

These, then, are some of the areas that need to be addressed by local writing centers and other members of the college or university. The principal mission of the visiting NWCA team would be to verify those reports and determine whether the writing center meets the criteria for accreditation at its appropriate level.

That raises another fairly complex question: what sorts of levels or ranks of accreditation should there be? SACS recognizes six levels of schools, ranging from those offering only associate degrees to those offering a doctorate in four or more fields. For writing centers, simply adopting that division could be problematic. It would be a mistake, for instance, to suggest that the writing center should be directed by a full-time specialist at a major research university but that the corresponding position at a community college might be filled otherwise. Instead, we might distinguish writing centers according to the number and kind of goals they espouse. A Level 1 writing center might concentrate largely on remediation and mastery of mechanical writing skills for writing classes and state-mandated exams. A Level 2 center would deal with these same concerns but add additional competencies and populations. As the levels progress, still other goals would be added, including such activities as developing scholarship and producing new knowledge in the discipline.

Although the classification and division exercise begun here is deliberately left unfinished, its general direction is reasonably clear. Such an approach would put writing centers in all sorts of schools on a more nearly equal footing than would a SACS-based approach. In addition, these divisions would help to point out that writing centers have much more potential than is often actualized because of limited visions of what a writing center is and does.

Ultimately, a comprehensive vision of what a writing center is and does—a vision of what a writing center *can* be and *can* do—will shape the accrediting process. My classification of writing centers is deliberately unfinished. Although I began with the most basic of writing center goals and left more advanced levels undefined, my choice doesn't suggest despair of defining those higher levels; instead, it is an invitation to collaboration on developing that comprehensive vision of the writing center. I hope that writing centers across the nation might agree upon a set of professional standards we all ought to strive to meet. My own utopian vision—at least at the moment—is of a writing center that is an autonomous entity, operating on its own budget and according to the agenda developed by its director, a writing-center specialist. Such a center would be staffed by a variety of professionals and students. Moreover, it would be a true *center*, serving the whole university community—working with students, staff, and faculty on a variety of tasks. This sort of center would address issues of writing instruction in all fields and be a clearinghouse for that sort of information.

After this brief look into my own private promised land, let me conclude by returning to the wilderness and suggesting some immediately practical advantages of establishing a national accrediting agency for writing centers.

First, simply trying to define and rank our varied goals in writing centers will help us to see more clearly who we are and what we are trying to do. The day-to-day work of writing centers is so demanding that we seldom have time to reflect on the larger purposes underlying that often frantic activity. Furthermore, even though we may acknowledge a diversity of approaches in writing centers, we seldom look beyond our own practices—unless it is to find how someone else deals with situations similar to our own.

That additional impetus to look beyond ourselves should come from our trying to formulate general accrediting standards; if we are ourselves being accredited, the requirement to formulate our own goals so that they can be evaluated locally by colleagues outside the writing center should be of great value as well. The process should help us clarify our own individual goals to ourselves; even if those goals and the objectives for achieving them are already written out, reviewing them will help reinforce them and perhaps suggest further modifications. Sending that material to other parts of the campus community will help to explain our mission to the rest of the school and win advocates in other departments.

Accreditation may also prove useful in helping us determine how to evaluate what we do, that long-standing problem of writing instruction in general. Although we should not expect definitive answers, a group of people working together on the problem of evaluation will be likelier to come up with more satisfactory near-answers than we have yet reached.

I am more optimistic in claiming the next benefit: a national accrediting agency should help improve writing centers across the country. Holding up a set of high standards ought to encourage centers to strive toward those standards in order to receive accreditation. These standards will also upgrade "professionalism" in staffing writing centers. As we see the multiplicity of our functions more clearly through these evaluations, we ought to see the need for thorough and diverse training. We are being asked increasingly to deal with a variety of populations with widely differing needs: in addition to the "traditional" student, we must also work with returning students, students with learning disabilities, students whose first language is not English, and so on. While the good will and patience of peer tutors and volunteers will go far in helping these students, they cannot replace specialized training for dealing with these difficulties.

Accreditation will also prove beneficial by focusing local administrative attention on writing centers in positive, constructive ways. Like the rest of the campus—and maybe even more—administrators need to be reminded of the goals and purposes of the writing center. If we can demonstrate to them that we are doing important instructional work—that we do not merely supplement classroom instruction—then we will be in a much better position to protect our program from budget cuts. If, through the accrediting process, we can demonstrate our role in recruiting and retention, we have a powerful argument for the value of the writing center, an argument in terms that administrators will understand. In short, we ought to use this process to build alliances with those who have administrative control over us. With enough evidence of this sort, it might be possible to make a case for treating the writing center as a separate program with an independent budget line, rather than making it a stepchild of an English department as it so often is.

Accreditation should bring with it some measure of status that will be helpful in a practical sort of way. Again, let me be cautious in making claims. Clearly, the sort of accreditation proposed here cannot have the same impact as SACS accreditation; after all, if a school does not meet SACS's criteria, it is pretty much out of business. However, there is a relevant connection with SACS. While SACS recognizes that separate units may be accredited by their own professional accrediting agencies, it is "the prerogative of the Commission to accept or reject the evaluations of such agencies"(2). Thus, even though we cannot make NWCA accreditation a condition for SACS accreditation, our criteria must be stringent enough to meet SACS criteria. Furthermore, SACS criteria specify that "a unit of an institution may be separately accredited if a significant portion of responsibility and decision-making authority for its educational activities lies within the unit and not in the other units of the institution or system"(6). Such separate SACS accreditation ought to be a goal of the autonomous center I have been describing. That day may be in the distant future, but, before it arrives, there are other advantages to be received. A school could use NWCA accreditation as part of its publicity describing what it can offer to prospective students. If that accreditation is at a higher level than might be expected for the school, its publicity value would be increased. For instance, a four-year school without a graduate program might conceivably boast a "better" writing center than a research university. Given the current concern for student writing instruction, this NWCA ranking would make a school look more attractive.

This ranking should make a writing center look more attractive to another important group of people outside the local campus—potential funding agencies. In light of the current financial climate for all schools, we are having to look increasingly to other sources of funding for our operations. In fact, the example of Cal State-Chico indicates the *necessity* of turning to those sources. Because that center is so widely regarded as a model program and cited extensively in the writing center literature, it should have less difficulty than many programs in gathering materials to document its effectiveness. The situation at Chico, though, ought to be a warning example to all of us. We cannot afford to ignore its implications.

The accrediting program sketched here would be an important step toward helping cope with the sorts of difficulties we face. I am all too well aware of the incompleteness of this initial proposal and the enormous complexity of reaching consensus on defining goals and assessing how well we have met them. Local administrators, too, will have to be convinced of the value—and the *validity*—of the accreditation. Despite these challenges, we ought to begin work on the project right away. After all, professionals regulate themselves, setting and enforcing standards appropriate to the task at hand. If we are professionals—as we claim—then we must assume those responsibilities.

Works Cited

Devet, Bonnie. "National Certification for a Writing Lab." *Writing Lab Newsletter* 17.2 (1992): 12-13.

Southern Association of Colleges and Schools. *Criteria for Accreditation*. Atlanta: Southern Association of Colleges and Schools, 1994.

Resisting the Editorial Urge in Writing Center Conferences: An Essential Focus in Tutor Training

Jane Cogie
Southern Illinois University

Muriel Harris, in her 1992 article "Collaboration is Not Collaboration is Not Collaboration," highlights one of the main problems writing center tutors face: "The struggle, as any tutor can confirm, is that we have to squelch our editorial urge to tinker with that paper and our human urge to help that writer sitting next to us turn in a better product" (373). Indeed, for tutors the tension between the desire to help students succeed in the short run and the challenge to help students become better writers in the long run is ongoing. Of course, so many elements of tutoring ask for attention that it is difficult for tutor trainers to know which issues to single out: the tutor's own ability to write? the rules of punctuation and grammar? listening and other interpersonal skills? knowledge of resources? strategies for helping students help themselves? multicultural concerns? Among the many issues clamoring for attention, the need to arm tutors with ways to resist the "editorial urge" must be a central emphasis in tutor training.

To help student writers genuinely improve, tutors need more than good intentions and more than a thorough versing in the qualities of good writing or tutoring techniques and theory. They must as well understand the distinction Stephen North makes between helping the writer and helping the writer's paper (438). And they must be able to recognize when the first has become the second. Helping tutors find strategies for assisting student writers is not enough. Tutors must also be sensitized to recognize when their focus has shifted away from the student.

This need can be met through a training sequence that allows tutors to internalize ways to involve students in their own writing. In the training program at Southern Illinois University, for instance, tutors move from collaborative peer group discussions of taped tutorials, to individual reflection on these discussions in a tutoring journal, to collaborative work with student writers, and then back to discussion and individual journal reflection. Not coincidentally, this sequence resembles the sequence through which tutees acquire effective writing processes: a sequence that moves from a collaborative tutoring session, to independent writing and revising, to in-class work, and back again for more collaboration and more independent writing. This training allows the tutor to internalize the types of dialogue that foster productive conferences much as the tutee internalizes the dialogue that fosters effective writing.

The essential components of this training are collaboration, listening, and written reflection. Each of these activities helps promote in tutors an awareness of themselves not as "little teachers," to use Kenneth Bruffee's term ("Training" 446), but as active participants in a learning community. They can then bring this awareness to bear in their future sessions with students.

Collaborative group discussions of observed sessions can help tutors give a more concrete shape to the theories they have learned and remind them of how productive dialogue can be. As Kenneth Bruffee has written, "To think well as individuals we must learn to converse well. The first steps to learning to think better, therefore, are learning to converse better and learning to establish and maintain the sorts of social context, the sorts of community life, that foster the sorts of conversation members of the community value" ("Collaborative" 640). Discussions among peer tutors about actual tutoring situations help to focus writing center problems and possible solutions. One tutor notes the usefulness of such collaborative work in the following journal entry:

> The discussion of sample tutor dialogues helped me see that the difference between a "good" and "poor" session is very fine, as is the line between doing students' papers for them and helping them learn skills to make better papers on their own. Being in a group discussion about the sample sessions, I was able to pinpoint some trouble spots in a tutorial and where they went wrong. On one occasion, I remember being tempted to agree with a student who voiced his disapproval of a professor's grading system. I wanted to agree with him simply because I wished to maintain our good working situation, but I remembered our discussion of a 'poor" tutorial in which a tutor had caused problems with that sort of behavior. I remembered that example and tried to get the student focused on his writing.

This tutor might have made the right decision without the benefit of peer discussion. Even if this had been the case, however, his desire for a positive relationship with his student might have caused him to hesitate in carrying out that decision.

Having tutors listen to their own taped sessions complements the collaborative work by allowing tutors to continue the conversation begun in the peer discussion and to come away with a further perspective on their own work. And it provides the element of showing, which is one essential of tutor training. While tutors benefit from learning the theories behind such key elements of their work as the writing process, collaborative conferencing, and determination of causes for writing problems, unless those tutors hear or observe how the theories play out in practice, they cannot truly understand the theories or their significance. Through listening to tapes of their own tutorials, tutors often come to realize how important effective attending skills are to tutoring. One tutor faces in his journal a concrete instance of a failure to attend closely: "In reviewing my taped session, I noticed that we were having a language-based communication breakdown at one point in the session, and I believe it might have been solved more quickly if I had listened a little more."

In this case, listening, combined with writing a journal response, gave the tutor a helpful distance from a problem in a previous session. And indeed written reflection by tutors on their collaboration and observation of sessions is an important complement to collaborative discussion. Janet Emig effectively suggests the uniqueness of written communication: "Because writing is often our representation of the world made visible, embodying both process and product, writing is more readily a form and source of learning than talking" (124). Writing gives our thoughts a separate existence, which, as Toby Fulwiler describes it, "allows us to interact with and modify them" (5). Tutors understand this quickly and sometimes remark on it in their journals:

> The journal helps get my thoughts out of my head and on to paper. For instance, I recognized problems one student was having, but I couldn't think of a solution. By writing down all my thoughts on the matter, I was able to formulate a plan to help her conquer her problem.

Writing in response to a taped session can also help tutors reflect on moments when they have shifted from helping the student to fixing the paper. One tutor responding in his journal wrote, "I felt I did come close to doing the work for the student, but for the most part I tried to lead him to discoveries." Such a recognition, when reinforced in writing, can help tutors sustain the necessary restraint.

Most tutor trainers would concede that it is a challenge to resist the temptation to fix the student's paper and genuinely involve students in tutoring sessions. Yet is it so central a challenge that it should consume a significant portion of the limited time available for tutor training? Yes, if the highly individualized interpersonal dynamics of conferences are to be preserved. Thomas Reigstad, who has examined how a group of writer-teachers acted when in conference with their students, has helpfully presented three models of conferencing: the teacher-centered model, in which the teacher dominates, asking only closed or leading questions; the collaborative model, in which the teacher involves the student writer in analyzing and solving writing problems; and the student-centered model, in which the student defines her or his writing problems and processes. Avoiding the fix-it shop approach need not mean following an exclusively student-centered model. It does require, however, becoming sensitized to the dynamics of conferences that keep the student writer involved.

To achieve these ends, trainers should give tutors the opportunity to learn elements of all three of Reigstad's models. Tutors also need to develop the listening skills for determining the approach best suited to the individual student as well as the facility to hear how well the approach is working. Some students, given the stage of their writing, may need tutors to direct their progress and may therefore learn most from conferences that are at least partially tutor-directed. Others will benefit from a more fully collaborative or student-centered model. Whatever tutoring mode is used, however, the focus must still be on the improvement of writers, not of papers. That goal must be central to tutor training since all three patterns can too easily deteriorate into an emphasis on product rather than process.

These tutor-training priorities are reinforced by Willa Wolcott's study of Reigstad's patterns as they apply to writing center tutoring. Wolcott studied seven graduate assistant writing center tutors in one-on-one sessions. All seven followed the teacher-centered conference model. The twelve conferences included in the study were "business-like," with "no attention to social courtesies" (18-19). And "'off-the-paper, exploratory talk' was rare"; "the tutors without exception directed the conferences" (20). Certainly, some of the students tutored in these twelve conferences might have benefited from a conference that was at least partially teacher-centered, but it is likely that some of them would have taken away more of lasting value had the session been more interactive.

Wolcott attributes the totally teacher-centered dynamics in these conferences to two factors: the limits of the half-hour sessions and the differences in age and education of the tutors and tutees. (The tutors were all experienced teachers in their thirties or forties.) Another contributing cause, though, may have been the brevity and nature of the tutors' training: "The tutors did not participate in any training program, but they were required to study a graduate manual and to read essays, such as Donald Murray's article on conferencing or chapters by Swift [sic] and Croft" (17). From Wolcott's description, the tutors appear to have had good intentions for involving the students: they used a variety of strategies, such as questioning to "engage the students in the dialogue" (20). And one tutor shows frustration with the lack of tutor-student interaction: "I try to be outgoing with those who sit passively. I'm uncomfortable with any one who just sits" (20). Had the reading done for training been followed by collaborative and reflective activities that reinforce the principles propounded, the tutors might have developed more resources for opening up dialogue with their students.

Are graduate assistants uniquely vulnerable to the teacher-centered model? Or is such a conferencing model common to undergraduate tutors as well? Unlike most undergraduates, graduate assistants usually are older and more educated than the students they tutor. In Wolcott's study in which such differences in age and education existed, a gulf between student and tutor seems evident. But does this mean that undergraduate tutors are immune to the hierarchical style of tutoring and that training for them need not focus on this issue? I would say no. The danger of falling too easily into a tutor-centered conference exists for them as well, for several reasons.

First, often those undergraduates chosen to tutor tend to be the very people most able to succeed within the traditional hierarchical teaching model, as John Trimbur points out in "Peer Tutoring: A Contradiction in Terms?"(22). Second, as Trimbur also indicates, uninitiated peer tutors are faced with a problem of allegiance (23). Pulled awkwardly between the role of peer and the role of professional, they believe they are expected to be buddies with the student and yet still have the knowledge and authority of a professional. Their allegiance divided, peer tutors have a great incentive to opt for the confidence-giving role of the professional, particularly if they have little experience with collaborative work.

Another factor that can prompt peer tutors and graduate students alike to succumb to tutor-centered tutorials is the inherently messy nature of collaboration in writing centers. As Andrea Lunsford has reminded us, collaboration is always a challenge "of power and control as constantly negotiated and shared," even outside the writing center (9). But, as Harris suggests, when one of the collaborators knows considerably more about writing and is not ultimately responsible for the writing done, as is usually the case in writing center collaborations, the challenge to sustain a genuinely constructive balance of power becomes even greater (371). Writing center tutors, involved with their students in what Harris terms "collaborative learning about writing," differ from others involved in "collaborative writing" (369); unlike collaborative writers, tutors "must focus on general writing skills." And with this focus they may have to deal with other instructional issues, such as the "writer's anxiety, poor motivation, cultural confusions, ineffective or dysfunctional composing strategies, lack of knowledge, or inability to follow assignment directions" (373). With instruction almost always involved to some degree or another in writing center collaboration, the desire to help the student in the short run becomes not only more tempting than usual but also more important to resist.

Given the difficult mix of collaboration and instruction involved, writing center tutoring is a particularly draining activity. As every tutor knows, conferencing with students demands action with very little lead time for deciding matters of cause, agenda, and strategy. The more tutors understand effective conferencing dynamics from the inside out, the less the pressure of time and the desire for visible progress will dominate. If tutor training programs include activities involving collaboration, listening, and reflective writing, they can help tutors—both graduate and undergraduate—keep the long-term needs of students uppermost and fend off the dangers of the "editorial urge."

Works Cited

Bruffee, Kenneth. "Collaborative Learning and the 'Conversation of Mankind.'" *College English* 46 (1984): 635-52.

—. "Training and Using Peer Tutors." *College English* 40 (1978): 432-49.

Emig, Janet. "Writing as Learning." *College Composition and Communication* 28 (1977): 122-28.

Fulwiler, Toby. *Teaching With Writing*. Portsmouth: Boynton/Cook, 1987.

Harris, Muriel. "Collaboration is Not Collaboration is Not Collaboration: Writing Center Tutorials vs. Peer-Response Groups." *College Composition and Communication* 43 (1992): 369-83.

Lunsford, Andrea. "Collaboration, Control, and the Idea of a Writing Center." *The Writing Center Journal* 12.1 (1991): 3-10.

North, Stephen. " The Idea of a Writing Center." *College English* 46 (1984): 433-46.

Reigstad, Thomas J. "Conferencing Practices of Professional Writers: Ten Case Studies." Diss. State Univ. of New York, Buffalo, 1980.

Trimbur, John. "Peer Tutoring: A Contradiction in Terms?" *The Writing Center Journal* 7.2 (1987): 21-27.

Wolcott, Willa. "Talking It Over: A Qualitative Study of Writing Center Conferencing." *The Writing Center Journal* 9.2 (1989): 15-29.

Assessing Writing Conference Talk: An Ethnographic Method

Carmen Werder
Roberta R. Buck

Western Washington University

We have completed two years of trying out a new method for assessing the performance of writing assistants in our writing center's conferences. We feel pleased with both the process and the results—not smug, but darn close. Our previous method was no method at all: we relied heavily on general impressions, sporadic eavesdropping, and arising crises to give us a vague sense of how our writing conferences were proceeding and what they were accomplishing. Like most other writing center personnel, we were consumed with the daily business of planning and doing. This absorption was especially comfortable because the notion of assessment seemed distasteful—partly because it would introduce a hierarchical element into an otherwise collegial environment and partly because it might mean having to address problems revealed in the process. Increasingly aware of the need for accountability, however, we realized we needed an assessment system.

Our method grew in response to a nagging sense that other methods for assessment are not adequate. The checklist methods of Flanders, Clark, and Reigstad and McAndrew (qtd. in Devet 75-76) seem rigid and pre-set. In isolating only certain features of writing conference dialogue, they seem to advocate ignoring everything else. Since our motive was to collect as much information as possible—a motive consistent with our underlying ethnographic principles—we wanted a method in which patterns emerge from data. In addition to excluding data, these checklist systems yield generalities not useful in specifying goals for improvement. We wanted a system in which identified needs directed future action.

Like checklist approaches, video methods (Hammermeister and Timms qtd. in Claywell 14) are equally unsatisfying although for different reasons. Our brief experience with video deepened our distaste for its use because it is both intimidating and intrusive. Additionally, information collected through video is unnatural and therefore suspect because video alters the nature of the conference being taped as both writing assistant and writer are apt to be self-conscious of being on-camera. Even if writing assistants were not unduly self-conscious during taping, viewing the tape with a supervisor present would likely be so uncomfortable that we could not imagine this scenario as promoting a pleasant affective climate for learning. Then, of course, there's the minor fact that our writing center owns no video equipment.

While less obtrusive, audio taping also has its drawbacks. In our experience, taped conferences prove useless without a follow-up transcription because there is no print record to examine. Anyone who has transcribed audio tapes knows it consumes hours of time. We would prefer that our writing assistants spend this time conferencing writers. Also, we wanted to devise a system that would allow writing assistants opportunities to observe each other. Since the written transcript was what we wanted, we needed a more direct and efficient method to obtain it.

Overview

Our decision to begin a systematic program of assessment, along with our determination to devise a better system, led to the discovery of our scheme. And it was a process of discovery. For instance, when we first initiated this assessment technique, we viewed it as a method we would simply repeat each quarter. Instead, it has evolved into a year-long sequential program that allows writing assistants to play an increasingly greater role in their own assessment. In our writing center, we are the two people responsible for instructing and supervising writing assistants, and, to begin with, we assumed all the responsibility for assessing. The first quarter, Roberta observed each assistant during a session and recorded the talk as completely as possible in a transcript. Then she analyzed the transcript, identifying the main patterns of strength. At a follow-up session, Carmen met with each assistant and, together, they set goals for the next quarter.

Rather than repeating the pattern identically the second quarter, we had assistants become more involved: Roberta again recorded the transcripts, but this time assistants completed the analysis of their own transcripts. Assistants took even more responsibility the third quarter, when they observed each other, completed their own analyses, and wrote closing self-assessments. Once these self-assessments were written, Carmen compiled information gained from quarterly written analyses, informal observations made throughout the year, and self-assessments and then wrote a final evaluation for each assistant.

Now, the system is set up so that writing assistants are responsible for the cycle of observation, analysis, and self-assessment each quarter.

Rationale

We had particular aims in mind when we devised our system. First, it needed to be open-ended. We didn't want to impose a sense of the ideal conference on our assistants; such is the limitation of predetermined checklists or categories. It is our experience that there is no one perfect method for guiding writing, so we were interested in identifying the patterns that would emerge in conference talk.

Second, the assessment experience needed to be affirming. Our intention was to put the emphasis on information and description rather than on evaluation and judgment. It is especially essential for this method to move from an identification of strengths because our writing center is staffed solely by student writing assistants who need to gain a professional sense of themselves.

Third, the system needed to be formative. Like writing and guiding writing, assessing writing assistants needs to be process-oriented. While we include a place for final, summative assessment, our emphasis is on providing a basis for regular and ongoing goal setting.

Finally, our design had to be tutor-centered. Because of our ethnographic approach to assessment, we didn't want assistants merely to be observed from a distance; rather, we wanted them to participate fully in discovering their own skills and goals. Furthermore, we know that if assistants see their own patterns emerge in the context of a particular session, they are more likely to internalize the principles of instruction that we emphasize.

Description

Our method of assessment has four steps—planning, observing, analyzing, and goal setting.

Planning

Observers make a schedule for assistants to sign up for times to be observed. Knowing in advance when they will be observed helps assistants prepare mentally and ensures that observations are scheduled at times when assistants actually have filled appointment slots. Giving assistants several times to choose from helps them feel more control over what initially may seem an intimidating event. To relieve anxieties, observers disclose as much as possible about what being observed entails; the more assistants know about the process, the less fearful they are about being observed.

Observing

Observers position themselves unobtrusively—near enough to the conference participants to hear, but out of the conference space so that they may observe the writing conference without interfering. Ideally, writing center clients will have no idea that they are part of a session being observed. (This is ethical because it is the assistants who are being observed.) Though some conferences last fifty minutes, observers needn't observe for more than thirty minutes. After a half hour, the pattern for the conference has been set; further transcription yields only a surfeit of data and writer's cramp.

Observers need only two pieces of equipment—blank paper and a pen. With these tools, observers transcribe as accurately as possible the conference talk—particularly assistant talk. Of course, it is impossible to write as fast as the participants talk, but there are usually times when observers can catch up—for example, while student-writers are reading their drafts or while they talk extensively about their topics. But recording every word is not as important as transcribing how sentences and questions are framed. How do assistants frame their questions? Their suggestions? Their clarifications? For example, observers can transcribe sentence frames like this: "When you say___X___, do you mean___X___?" The blank is given to stand for quotations lifted from the draft or for content glosses. (See Appendix transcript for examples of this coding technique.) Talk about draft content does not really give much information about the assistant; more important is how the assistant introduces and continues conference talk.

After being observed, assistants typically display some curiosity about how observers perceived the conference talk. To ease assistants' anxieties, observers may make transcripts immediately available to assistants for their quick review. Observers, however, refrain from making interpretive comments at this point—it is far too early in the process for judgments.

Analyzing

Observers will want to examine the data (transcripts) for strengths, preferably while conferences are fresh. Rereading transcripts and looking for conference patterns, observers make a mental note of phrases that seem to be repeated often. Recurring language such as "Do you think you could___X___?" or "Here you've said___X___" often signals a significant pattern. If these patterns represent a strength, and quite often they do, observers mark the beginning of the phrase with a colored pen. (See Appendix transcript for an example of this kind of analysis.) Every phrase indicative of a particular strength is marked with the same color pen. On another sheet, a key explains the strength associated with that color. (See Appendix for examples of identified strengths.) For each assistant, observers identify up to three strengths.

Before passing on transcripts and recorded strengths, observers write brief notes providing overall impressions of assistants and their conferences. These notes express what the conference talk cannot capture. For example, if an assistant exudes a particular confidence or rapport, or if, on the other hand, an assistant seems tentative or controlling, these impressions are noted. Observers pass these notes along with all conference data to the person who will be guiding the goal-setting conference.

Goal Setting

As soon as assistants have had observations, they sign up for thirty-minute sessions to review their transcripts. These conferences can occur during their regularly scheduled hours when they have no appointments. The supervisor prepares for these conferences by glancing over the observers' overall impressions and the analyses of the strengths (if they have already been completed) and by gathering previous assessment records. It is not necessary for the supervisor to read the observations thoroughly beforehand, but it does help to scan them to get a general sense of assistants' profiles.

After receiving the transcription notes and analysis of strengths, the person conducting the goal-setting conference meets with assistants to review together their assessment records. While experienced assistants can successfully observe and analyze conference talk once they have received some instruction, the goal-setting conference requires more experience in facilitation and thus is more appropriate for a supervisor who has had some teaching experience.

When supervisor-assistant conferences begin, the supervisor reminds assistants that the purpose of these meetings is to pinpoint patterns of strength in the transcripts and to list goals for the future. Then the supervisor and the assistant read the transcripts aloud. Assistants read their parts, and the supervisor reads the role of student-writers. As they read the transcripts, assistants watch for patterns that emerge in the transcripts and mark those places for discussion later. If an analysis has already been done, together they review the strengths listed. If an analysis has not yet been done, the assistant takes time to record patterns of strength.

Once the strengths have been recorded, the supervisor usually asks if any of the skills come as a surprise. This question gives assistants an opportunity to highlight strengths they were unaware of, to acknowledge ones they have been actively cultivating, and to confirm what certain skills actually look/sound like. If the supervisor observes any additional strengths, she asks assistants to add them to the list in their own words.

Sometimes, assistants want to discuss their patterns of need first. If the assistant is generally confident, beginning with goals and then moving to strengths can work. However, if the supervisor senses that assistants need to build on a foundation of successes, then she steers them in that direction first. Typically, assistants eagerly note two to three strengths and then quite naturally move to areas they are not satisfied with. Curiously, acknowledging strengths often directly reveals areas of need. For example, an assistant might note that she now asks more open-ended questions, allowing the student to maintain authorship. But she might also note that by asking so many questions, she is not allowing students enough time to think. Therefore, she might make it her goal to leave more response time for questions asked. One virtue of this assessment system is that by acknowledging a strength first, the assistant is more likely to recognize a related need.

Striking are the rigor and accuracy that assistants bring to this goal-setting phase. Rarely do they resist acknowledging areas of need, so rarely will the supervisor need to designate specific goals; in fact, assistants often have much more insight into their own areas for improvement than supervisors might have. Once the skills and goals have been recorded and attached to the transcript, assistants compare them with previous records: highlighting former goals that have now become strengths, underscoring recurrent patterns of either strengths or goals, and exploring specific strategies for achieving goals listed. After the sessions, photocopies are made of the assessment records, so the assistants have their own copies for reference, especially for writing self-assessments at the close of the quarter.

Implications

Our assessment system has implications for generating personnel files, refining curricula, and revising writing center programs. The information gathered in the process of assessment generates a written performance record that can be useful when an assistant's performance proves inadequate. In the worst case, these records can be used to support disciplinary actions, including dismissal. While we have never had to use the system this way, we need to be prepared for such dire possibilities. On the other hand, we have routinely used these records as a basis for writing letters of recommendation. They are a rich source of information, complete with examples detailing specific skills.

In addition to creating personnel files, this system informs the educational curriculum for our assistants. The transcripts reveal those elements of instruction that assistants already practice and those elements that they have not yet put into place. For example, we discovered that, despite our fervent emphasis, most assistants were not getting whole drafts read at the beginning of conferences so that they could not move from global to local issues. This revelation prompted us to demonstrate the inadequacy of their approach and present specific strategies for resolving this problem. Not only do transcripts reveal areas of need in assistant education, they also become materials that can be used in practicums. For example, selected transcripts are now included in our anthology of required readings, giving assistants samples of language patterns that facilitate conferences and those that interfere with them.

Finally, this system contributes to a more complete understanding of writing center programs. The process of contrasting the actual with the ideal defines who we are as a writing center and clarifies our vision of who we want to be. Instead of assuming that our conferences do what we hope, the system documents what they actually do and, in the process, reveals more about our audience and its needs. For example, one of the things we found out in reviewing transcripts is that many writing conferences dealt with reading challenges, so we have revised our curriculum to include strategies for guiding reading.

Conclusion

This assessment system responds to the need that writing centers have to be accountable. Unlike checklists, transcripts expand our understanding of effective strategies for guiding writing. Unlike video taping, this ethnographic method preserves the authenticity of writing conferences. And unlike audio taping, this manual transcription method provides a more immediate record of writing conference talk. By minimizing the hierarchical nature of the assessment relationship, the system comfortably responds to our natural desire for feedback. The result is that we all become observers and participants in the process of guiding literacy.

Works Cited

Claywell, Gina. "Nonverbal Communication and Writing Lab Tutorials." *Writing Lab Newsletter* 18.7 (1994): 13-14.

Devet, Bonnie. "A Method for Observing and Evaluating Writing Lab Tutorials." *The Writing Center Journal* 10.2 (1990): 75-83.

Appendix:
Sample Observation Transcript

Note: Because of publication restraints, we have replaced the color coding with asterisks.

Assistant: H.
Date: 2/7/94
Class: Theatre 201

H: So you're working on a second draft?

S: Yeah. I have a 1st draft.

H: How many points is this worth?

S: I got -4 points.

H: So you wanted to ... what?

S: (Silence)

H: What's the main thing you're working on?

S: Compare and contrast our opinion against reviewer.

H: O.K. Now I've worked w/this assignment before. Is this your 1st para?

S: No, I have 2 para. 1st and 2nd assignment. But there's no ending.

H: So you're kind of confused about your conclusion?

S: Yeah.

H: You might want to ask the teacher. Did you get any comments? (Reads comments) "Need to work on grammar and transitions." *What we usually do here is have you read it out loud because (gives rationale). So if you could read it and I'll be writing notes.

S: (Reads 1st para. Stops. Then continues when H. doesn't comment.)

H: **After reading that, did anything strike you?

S: Yeah. Some things seem choppy. And I became redundant.

H: Why don't you put a little mark by all the places you notice and we'll come back to them. So in this first part, I see you're trying to ___X___ and in the 2nd part you're trying to ___X___. Right?

S: Yeah. Does that make sense?

H: Yeah, it makes sense and it meets the assignment. Now for a conclusion an idea might be to restate your idea. Maybe next we could go back to some of the sentences that seemed to have problems. *I'm just going to go thru myself and read this to myself and I'll stop when I see problems. (Pause) Now here you need to be uniform. You could either add something here or delete this. **Now here's a sentence you marked. What did you think?

S: Well it's like two different ideas in the same sentence.

H: Yes, maybe you're trying to say too much. I guess I'm a ***little confused about your meaning, so could you just tell me what you're trying to say—the two main points of this sentence?

S: (Talks)

H: So "the need to repent" and "time barrier"?

S: Yeah.

H: ***So are you saying ___X___?

S: (Explains)

H: O.K. I think we should work on either making it two sentences or … I don't know. I guess when you explained it it made more ***sense. I should have written it down. (Pause)

S: (Explains again)

H: I guess for me to understand it as a reader …. Are you trying to make a connection between these two ideas?

S: Yeah.

H: I think this might be what is confusing me, this in the past. Maybe you could even put a period.

S: Oh! So I could do ___X___?

H: Yeah.

S: (Writes)

H: Hmm … I wonder if you could put a transition there.

S: What's a transition?

H: Oh. No problem. Lots of people don't know. (Gives examples)

S: What about "incidentally"?

H: I might try a "therefore" because you sort of have a cause and effect. If you're going to ... if you ... you might what to check your tense there.

S: Oh, did I really mess up on those?

H: No, not really. Just the once. **Okay, so he thinks the theme is ___X___ and you think the theme is ___X___. Now did you have another thing you marked? Oh, this "child."

S: Lots of "childs."

H: **Do you remember the name? If you want to change that, you could come up with another word.

S: How about if I ___X___?

H: Yeah, that'd work good. (Reads a sentence.)

S: Did I lose you?

H: Yeah. What do you mean?

S: I could ___X___?

H: Yeah. ***Here's a sentence that's a little vague. What does it mean?

S: (Explains)

H: Maybe if you could add something like you just said it would be a little clearer.

S: O.K.

H: I wonder ... this construction is a little awkward. (Reads sentence) Is that it? Could you ...

S: Is it really awkward?

H: Yeah. I don't know how to explain why this doesn't work. Sorry.

S: ***(Explains what she was trying to do in the sentence)

H: Maybe you could say ... well you could maybe not use a ";" because you should have a complete thought. So if you said___X___. Does that make sense?

S: (Writes down what H says)

H: So that way you keep the focus you want and it's grammatically correct. So this part here is about ___X___?

S: Yeah.

H: You might want to add a sentence to say that it's all going to be about___X___. Because now I see it, but only because you just told me.

S: O.K.

H: ***By this sentence, I take it you mean___X___?

S: Yes, first ... because I'm trying to do___X___.

H: Oh, I thought it meant ___X___. Like I said, there are a few sentence structure difficulties. But I do think you've met the assignment. Any last minute "??"

S: I think I'm going to sign up for another appointment for another paper.

Transcript Analysis

Strengths:
* Makes explicit writing center procedures and the rationales for those procedures.

** Encourages independence by prompting the student to identify and suggest corrections to the problems she sees in her own work.

*** Gives the student plenty of "air time" to talk through her ideas and to state her intentions.

Goals:
—Spend more time verifying thesis before moving to local concerns.

—Ask more open-ended questions when dealing with local concerns (instead of recommending changes to the writer). Try using more "what" questions.

Using Collaborative Groups to Teach Critical Thinking

Jean Kiedaisch
Sue Dinitz

University of Vermont

In our work with writing across the curriculum, we've noticed that more and more faculty who teach introductory courses view themselves as introducing students to a discipline's way of thinking. Instead of presenting students with conclusions reached by, for example, historians or sociologists, these faculty teach their students how historians create history or how sociologists reach conclusions about society. A professor in one such course at the University of Vermont, William Mierse, emphasizes process rather than product in his introductory art history course. Rather than having students memorize trays of slides, he has them create interpretations of works of art. To construct their own interpretations, students need to learn some of the discipline's key critical thinking skills:

(1) how to look at a work of art—to notice the choices the artist has made, to see what questions are posed by the work and how to answer them;
(2) how to focus their complex responses into a manageable argument;
(3) how to use supporting evidence to make their argument;
(4) how differing responses lead to differing interpretations— that there is no one right interpretation.

Like other such teachers, Professor Mierse feels he can best teach these thinking skills through a formal writing assignment. While journals and class discussions allow students to note their initial responses and begin to develop an interpretation, only in a formal paper are students forced to construct a clear, coherent, fully developed argument. So Professor Mierse assigns papers in this course, even though it enrolls from 60 to 120 students. Further, he believes that just assigning the writing won't accomplish his goals, that he should help students learn how to engage in the critical thinking described above.

So Professor Mierse turned to the Writing Center for help with this assignment. But what he wanted from the Writing Center was very different from the services we'd provided to writing–intensive courses previously, when individual students worked with a tutor to improve a draft, either before or after the professor had seen it. Professor Mierse wanted students to come in groups, with the tutor acting as a facilitator. And he wanted them to come in before they'd written a draft—to get help with the thinking that goes into producing it, not with revision. Why facilitated groups for teaching critical thinking? And why writing tutors? We'd like to discuss why by looking at excerpts from two sessions.

Both groups are interpreting a fifteenth–century relief, *Nativity with Two Magi,* located in the University of Vermont's Fleming Museum. This first excerpt is from early in a session. Kirsten, a student, has just noted that artists don't usually show Mary lying down in a birthing position. Abbie, the tutor, responds:

Abbie: What about, um, that's true of the other works that you've seen? ...
Robin: The ones that we've seen, like in the book, I looked at the other pieces and, Mary, they're, none of them ...
Kirsten: Right, she's ...
Robin: She's always standing up. [Abbie: Ah]
Kirsten: Right, very strong, kinda like not ...
Gail: She doesn't look very glorified in this. [Kirsten: No.] Usually she does.
Kirsten: Right, she's looking off.
Robin: But, she is, her figure's larger though than the other figures, the wisemen.
Kirsten: Yeah, it's bigger. [Robin: Yeah] Yeah.
Abbie: Now why would you say she's not glorified?
Gail: Well, I just, every time I've seen Mary before she has ... this presence where she kinda just looks glorified, like she has those things behind her, you know. I don't know what they're called.
Robin: Like halos, like?
Gail: Yeah.
Robin: Rays of light or something.
Kirsten: She's more human here.
Gail: In this one, yeah, she's lying. Usually, usually it's just her face, or if it's her body, it's usually, I've never seen her lying down and like, you see her whole body, before ...
Susan: I think her pose is rather, lavish, I mean she's like lounging,

Kirsten: Yeah, she's pouring herself.

Robin: She reminded me of Cleopatra or something, when you said that. [Kirsten: Yeah, yeah]

Gail: It doesn't look like what she normally looks like.

Abbie: In terms of, you bring up Cleopatra, in terms of the style, do you see any style or distinct, the Egyptian style or the way she's posed or why she reminds you of Cleopatra?

Robin: Her pose, I don't know why, she seems like she's ... the wisemen are all around her and they're bowing down to her, you know ...

Kirsten: But I wasn't really clear if they were bowing to her or to Baby Jesus?

Robin: Baby Jesus, yeah, but doesn't it seem like, he's, he's at the top, [Kirsten: Right] and she's next to him

Kirsten: And it's more like they're focusing their attention on her

Robin: Yeah, cause they're on the same level

Kirsten: 'Cause neither of them seem to know that they're here .... Baby Jesus and Mary are staring off, they appear to be looking at the same thing ... they're like contemplating, they're more passive [Robin: Yeah]

Peter: Yeah ... did you look at their eyes?

Kirsten: Yeah, I did.

Peter: 'Cause their eyes are all staring off into nowhere.

What we first noticed was how the students' view of the presentation of Mary is enriched through this discussion. Gail notes that Mary does not look very glorified in the piece. Robin challenges this observation, noting that Mary's figure is larger than the others. Abbie asks the group to explain why they'd say she's not glorified. As everyone contributes observations, the group ends up noting how Mary *is* glorified— Cleopatra–like—with the wisemen bowing down to her as she looks off in the distance.

Interestingly, this idea—that Mary is glorified—becomes the focus of the paper written by Gail (who initially said Mary doesn't look glorified), which begins as follows:

The Nativity with two Magi, in Fleming Museum, is part of a narrative frozen in time. The narrative is the story of the birth of baby Jesus when the magi come to bring him gifts of gold, myrrh and frankincense. The artist is taking this moment of time to demonstrate the divinity of Jesus and his mother the Virgin Mary. This is done by having the eyes of Jesus and Mary focus away from the scene making them appear distant and not involved in their surroundings.

When she left the session, Gail had no idea that she was going to focus on the divinity of Mary. At the end, Abbie asks the group, "So, how are you feeling about paper topics?" and Gail responds, "I don't know what I'm going to do it on. I really have to go back and look at it." During her interview with Jean, Gail reveals that she had been considering writing about the role of the animals, not Mary:

> What I wrote I didn't bring up in the discussion because I thought of it afterward. The group got me thinking in the right pattern. I brought up an idea about the ox and the ass. I said something about how they relate to the Bible. Abbie said, "You could say that, but you'd need good evidence." So I wondered how I could do that. Then I noticed the eyes of Mary and Jesus and how they were looking off. So the discussion told me I had to go look at the piece for a long time.

The session motivates Gail to go back to the piece and get more support for a thesis about the ox and the ass. But when she starts looking, she focuses on the eyes, an idea that she seems to think of as original, apparently unaware that it came from the group discussion. Still, she recognizes the value in listening to other students' ideas. When asked, "Was talking with others helpful, or would a meeting just with the tutor have been better?" she responds:

> Definitely talking with others. For the first paper I missed the session, so I went and talked with him ... talking with Professor Mierse was helpful, but not as much, because he wasn't giving me any ideas. He just said "What do you think? What do *you* think?" I got five people's ideas in the group. Some of the things people said, I never would have thought of.

Some teachers might be worried about students' getting ideas from one another, thinking it constitutes plagiarism. In the interview, Gail suggests why this needn't be a worry. To the question "How difficult did writing this kind of paper seem to you?" she answers, "After our session, I went back and sat looking at the piece for an hour. The ideas people had, they weren't my own ideas, so I didn't understand them that well. I couldn't have backed them up." Even though she draws on the ideas in the group, Gail realizes she has to think them through herself. Her thesis and supporting ideas end up being very different from those of the others in her group.

Interestingly, another group (tutored by Karen) has a similar discussion, which leads one writer to a very different view of Mary. Debbie begins this discussion by pointing out that Mary's position, reclining in a barn, doesn't fit the story as told in the gospels:

Debbie: But also what interested me was ... one of the questions asked about like comparing it to the gospel story [Karen: Uh hum] and um, in the gospel story like um Jesus is like in a barn with like swaddling clothes and like here she's reclining. [Karen: Ya]

Renee: Could you find that in the gospel? 'Cause I looked at it, I looked in the gospel, because I'm in a Bible seminar, and I couldn't find it written, at all, it was just written ...

Karen: In Luke?

Renee: Yeah, but all it said in Luke was that they were going to go to the inn and it was full so they went to the manger instead ...

Debbie: Yeah, but there wouldn't, still there's no place in the barn to recline, you know, like in ...

Karen: You mean to recline like you were some sort of princess?

Debbie: Right, right. [Karen: OK] So it takes the realism, like makes her seem more divine which, I don't know ...

Jen: Kinda weird, I didn't see her as divine in this picture. I saw her as sort of, well, this is kind of well, a little bit brazen. I mean, well, she's a little bit slutty in this position. She's like, her position, is, like ...

Karen: Sort of Mae Westish? Come on up and see me sometime?

Jen: Right, yeah, I don't know maybe that's ...

Karen: Yeah, it's just a different way of seeing things.

Renee: And there was also like she was draped but there was subtle like curves so you could see underneath [Jen: Yeah, yeah] underneath the drapery, like hinting toward her sexuality, which is interesting because she's supposed to be the Virgin Mary.

Jen: Was she a virgin?

Karen: I don't know.

Here again, we see one student (Jen) challenging another's (Debbie's) view of Mary. Then we see Renee go on to support and help develop Jen's view. In this discussion, Karen, the tutor, is able to emphasize that one interpretation isn't right and another wrong—they're just different ways of seeing.

Through this discussion, Jen gains confidence in her interpretation. The point becomes a major one in her paper, which compares the relief to an Islamic piece:

> In addition, Mary is portrayed in the Islamic artistic style by the way in which she exudes sexuality through the folds of her chiseled wooden drapes. Her femininity is accentuated through the lines of the cloth which cling to and encircle her hips and breasts.

In her interview, Jen reports that having her idea challenged was helpful to her. When asked, "Did you find the group session helped you with writing your paper?" she responds: "The second session helped me by challenging my thesis, getting into the art .... It was helpful to talk to other people ... just talking to anyone, to get feedback and be challenged."

What do we see happening in these two excerpts that encourages critical thinking? First, the group gives students an opportunity to ask questions (Kirsten: I wasn't really clear if they were bowing to her or to Baby Jesus? Renee: Could you find that in the gospel?) and share observations (about the position of Mary, the passage in the gospel, where the eyes are focused). The ensuing discussion enriches students' views of how Mary is portrayed in the relief; each group ends up expressing a different view of Mary from the one they started with—one group switches from not glorified to divine, the other from divine to sexual. As they challenge each other's ideas, they strengthen and gain confidence in their own interpretations. This discussion of Mary helps Gail find a focus (that the artist is demonstrating the divinity of Mary) and helps Jen and Gail develop support for their theses (Jen uses the idea about Mary's sexuality to draw a parallel to an Islamic piece; Gail uses the observation about the eyes to support her thesis). After the session, Gail is motivated to continue looking at the piece to further develop and support her interpretation.

In comparing the thinking done in these excerpts with the critical thinking skills Professor Mierse is trying to develop, we see a close match: the students do seem to be learning how to look, how to focus, how to develop and support. So the tapes convinced us of the value of the group discussion. But was the tutor necessary? Couldn't Professor Mierse have divided his class into groups and given them time for discussion? We looked at the excerpts above to see what roles the tutor plays in the group.

The tutor asks several kinds of questions—questions that stimulate discussion (Abbie: That's true of the other works that you've seen?); questions that help students clarify their ideas (Karen: You mean to recline, like you were some sort of princess?); and questions that help students develop support for their interpretation (Abbie: Now why would you say she's not glorified?). Much of the tutor talk is monosyllabic (Ah, uh huh, yeah, ok), which seems meant to encourage students to express and more fully formulate their ideas. And, finally, Karen frames the discussion with the observation that different interpretations are acceptable.

In the sessions as a whole, the tutor plays additional roles. She organizes how the group spends its time. She keeps the group focused, first on discussing the work of art and then on developing their individual arguments. (Both tutors end the session by going around and asking students to describe their plan for the paper.) She asks direct questions to help students focus their papers (Abbie: That's very interesting. If you were to write about something like that in your paper, how would you go about it?). The tutor manages the discussion, stimulating it when it slows and synthesizing ideas when things get messy. For example, after a long discussion about the ox and the ass at the top of the relief, Abbie brings together all the possible explanations:

> And it all leads to one impression you know, and yet it could be the horns that top off the pyramid, or it could be the human-izing aspect of Christ, it could be, like you said, with the quote [from Isaiah] symbolizing the people, you know, the followers … and if you decided to discuss the animals above Christ you could bring all of these things into it.

Finally, the tutor makes sure conflict isn't suppressed or that a few people don't dominate the group.

Do writing center tutors need any special training to facilitate group discussions? Managing the group interaction does involve some skills beyond those needed for individual sessions. For example, in individual sessions, tutors can determine where a student is in the writing process and then negotiate an agenda; in group sessions, students may be at different places in the writing process, complicating the setting of an agenda. In individual sessions, quiet students can be questioned directly by the tutor; in group sessions, these students need to be drawn into an ongoing conversation with their peers. In individual sessions, tutors don't encounter conflicts between students; in group sessions, such conflicts often emerge when students present differing views.

To develop new strategies, the tutors watch a tape of a group session and discuss how the tutor interacts with the group. And the new tutors meet with experienced tutors to discuss the differences between tutoring individuals and facilitating groups.

Having students discuss their ideas in a group session before writing a draft seems to us an exciting way to teach critical thinking—

through conversations with their peers, the more experienced students take their ideas further than they would have on their own, and the less experienced students are drawn into the conversation and learn how to engage in it. And, whereas required individual sessions often create some resistance, students seem almost uniformly to enjoy these group sessions. Semester after semester, about 90% of the students say in their course evaluations that seeing a tutor helped them improve the quality of their papers, and 90–95% recommend that the writing tutors be used in the next year's art history courses.

These sessions benefit not only the students but also our writing center. Many of the students come back for individual sessions once they've written their papers. And this combination—requiring group sessions and making individual sessions optional—is more efficient and economical than setting up individual appointments for entire classes.

Upon hearing about the group sessions, other faculty have begun thinking more creatively about how to use our writing center. A literature professor who assigns a collaboratively written midterm asked if the groups could meet with a tutor. Groups began coming from introductory writing courses to work not only on collaborative interpretive essays but also on collaborative research essays and on editing. So we are all beginning to think of the writing center in a new way—not just as a place where individual students can get help with their writing, but also as a place where critical thinking can be fostered through facilitated group interaction.

Notes on Contributors

Jacob S. Blumner is a doctoral student in rhetoric and composition at the University of Nevada. His research interests emphasize writing centers, developmental writing, writing across the curriculum, and assessment.

Roberta R. Buck is Program Manager of the University Writing Programs at Western Washington University, where, in addition to her duties in the Writing Center, she also teaches composition to nonnative English speakers. She has recently conducted research examining the effects on revision of teachers' written feedback in contrast to peer-tutor writing conference feedback, and she is currently preparing the results of this study for publication.

Kathleen Shine Cain has taught composition and literature for over twenty years and has served as Director, Associate Director, and steering committee member for the Merrimack College Writing Center during the past nine years. She has given presentations on writing center theory and pedagogy as well as on collaborative learning and literature at CCCC, NCTE, NWCA, the National Peer Tutoring in Writing Conference, and the New England Writing Centers Association conference. She is a past Chair of the New England Writing Centers Association and has served on that organization's steering committee. Her publications include *Rough Drafts: A Workbook* (Prentice Hall, 1990); *The Allyn & Bacon Workbook* (1992); *Exploring Literature: A Collaborative Approach*, with Albert C. DeCiccio and Michael J. Rossi (Allyn & Bacon, 1993); and *Living in the USA: Readings for Critical Thinking and Writing* (Allyn & Bacon, 1994).

Jane Cogie, formerly director of the Learning Skills Center at Cornell College, currently directs the Writing Center at Southern Illinois University at Carbondale. She has recently given conference presentations on tutor training and on the effects of tutoring on teaching.

Albert C. DeCiccio has taught primarily rhetoric and composition for fifteen years, has served as Director, Associate Director, and steering committee member for the Merrimack College Writing Center during the past nine years, and is currently Dean of the Faculty of Liberal Arts at Merrimack College. He has given presentations on writing center theory and practice as well as on social constructionism and collaborative learning at CCCC, NCTE, NWCA, the National Peer Tutoring in Writing Conference, and the New England Writing Centers Association conference. He has been a member of the Editorial Board of *The Writing Center Journal*, and he regularly contributes articles to *Writing Lab Newsletter*. His books include *Sample Research Papers from Across the Disciplines* (HarperCollins, 1991) and *Exploring Literature: A Collaborative Approach*, with Kathleen Shine Cain and Michael J. Rossi (Allyn & Bacon, 1993).

Sue Dinitz teaches composition and co-directs the writing center at the University of Vermont. She has presented at CCCC and regional and national writing center conferences and published in *The Writing Center Journal* and *The Journal of Teaching Writing*.

Dawn M. Formo is a Ph.D. candidate in the Rhetoric, Linguistics, and Literature Program in the English Department at the University of Southern California. She teaches writing at USC and at Long Beach City College. In the fall of 1995, she begins an assistant professorship in the Literatures and Writing Studies Program at California State University–San Marcos.

Julie Hagemann recently joined the English and Philosophy Department at Purdue University Calumet in Hammond, Indiana, where she coordinates the basic writing program and works closely with the Writing Tutorial Lab. She is a former director of the Writing Center at the University of Alabama in Tuscaloosa and a former acting coordinator of Writing Tutorial Services at Indiana University in Bloomington. She also taught composition at the University of Alabama in Birmingham.

Cynthia Haynes-Burton is Assistant Professor in the School of Arts and Humanities at the University of Texas at Dallas, where she teaches both graduate and undergraduate rhetoric, composition, and electronic pedagogy. As Director of Rhetoric and Writing, she manages a networked computer classroom and directs the first-year undergraduate Rhetoric program. Her publications have appeared in *Pre/Text*, *Composition Studies*, *Writing Center Journal*, and *Writing Lab Newsletter*. She is currently working on book chapters for collections on textual-based virtual reality, feminism and pedagogy, cyberspace and teaching, writing and ethics, keywords in composition, and writing centers and rhetoric. In addition, she is Guest Editor of a forthcoming special double issue of *Pre/Text* on "Virtual Rhetorics." She is a member of the Executive Committee of AEE (Alternative Education Environments) and co-founder of Lingua MOO, a text-based virtual synchronous learning environment for UT Dallas students and faculty.

Dave Healy directs the Reading & Writing Center at the University of Minnesota's General College. He also edits *The Writing Center Journal*. His research interests include the professional role orientation of writing center directors, computers and composition, and online writing centers.

His work has appeared in *The Writing Center Journal, WPA: Writing Program Administration, Computers and Composition, College ESL, Teaching English in the Two-Year College,* and other journals.

Robert W. Holderer is Assistant Professor of Writing and Director of the Center for Writing at Edinboro University of Pennsylvania. He has twenty-three years of experience teaching composition and literature at all levels. He received his Ph.D. in writing assessment at Oklahoma State University. In addition to publications and presentations on writing assessment, he has published on censorship and the religious right. His article "The Religious Right: Who Are They and Why Are We the Enemy?" will appear in *English Journal* this year.

Wangeci JoAnne Karuri left Nairobi, Kenya, in 1992 to study at Coe College in Cedar Rapids, Iowa. Currently in her senior year, Wangeci is an honors student working toward a double major in computer science and sociology, and an art minor. Wangeci has worked as a peer consultant in the Coe Writing Center since her freshman year. She is also actively involved in student affairs and residential life at Coe. Although she plans to pursue a career in architecture, Wangeci has a strong interest in writing. She has been involved in two literary publications at Coe College, *The Pearl* and *Mwendo,* for which she has been an assistant editor and editor, respectively.

Jean Kiedaisch teaches composition and co-directs the Writing Center at the University of Vermont. She has presented at CCCC and regional and national writing center conferences and published in *The Writing Center Journal* and *The Journal of Teaching Writing.*

Joe Law is the Assistant Director of the William L. Adams Writing Center at Texas Christian University. His research interests include writing centers, Victorian studies, and connections among the arts. He has published essays on writing instruction, literature, and music in such journals as *Review of English Studies, Composition Studies, Yearbook of Interdisciplinary Studies in the Fine Arts, The Opera Quarterly,* and *Twentieth Century Literature.* With Christina Murphy, he edited *Landmark Essays on Writing Centers* (Hermagoras, 1995). He is the South Central Writing Centers Association representative on the Executive Board of the National Writing Centers Association. He is Associate Editor of *English in Texas* and *Composition Studies.*

Donna Fontanarose Rabuck is the Assistant Director of the Writing Skills Improvement Program, an award-winning academic support program for minority and economically disadvantaged students at the University of Arizona. She has held this position for eleven years and serves as the on-site coordinator of the various components of the Writing Skills Program. She is also the Assistant Director of the Summer Institute for Writing and Thinking, a minority recruitment and outreach program that she, Roseann Gonzalez, and John Rabuck created ten years ago to attract minority high school students to higher education and to provide teachers of all disciplines with knowledge of and practice in writing. She received her Ph.D. in English from Rutgers University and also teaches composition courses at Pima College's Community campus.

Cheryl Reed teaches composition as an adjunct instructor at San Diego Mesa and Miramar community colleges in San Diego, California. She is at present looking for ways to help students negotiate changes brought about in the world of work by continuous innovations in science, computer, and video technologies. She has published book reviews in *Studies in Psychoanalytic Theory* and is currently completing a dissertation on nineteenth-century apparitional folklore. This essay grew out of dialogues with tutors and writing instructors at various institutions and was conceived while she was employed as a teaching assistant in one of five writing programs at the University of California, San Diego.

Michael J. Rossi has taught composition, business communication, and literature for over twenty years, has served as Director, Associate Director, and steering committee member for the Merrimack College Writing Center during the past nine years, and recently completed six years as Chair of the Department of English at Merrimack. He has given presentations on writing center practice and collaborative learning at CCCC, NCTE, NWCA, the National Peer Tutoring in Writing Conference, and the New England Writing Centers Association conference. He has served on the steering committee of the New England Writing Centers Association. His publications include "Analysis of the Writing Process" in *Conducting Research in Business Communication,* with Joan Rossi (Association for Business Communication, 1988) and *Exploring Literature: A Collaborative Approach,* with Kathleen Shine Cain and Albert C. DeCiccio (Allyn & Bacon, 1993).

Joseph Saling directed the Writing Labs at Massachusetts Bay Community College in Wellesley Hills, Massachusetts, from 1989 to 1995. Prior to joining the faculty at MBCC he was director of the Writing Center at Marshall University in West Virginia, and was also the Writing Specialist on the English faculty at St. Anselm College in New Hampshire. He did his graduate work in English at Ohio State University. In May of 1995, he left teaching to devote full time to his own writing, though he remains active in writing center activities.

David E. Schwalm was writing program administrator at Arizona State University Main from 1986-92. Since the fall of 1992, he has served as Vice Provost for Academic Programs at Arizona State University West.

Steve Sherwood is the Coordinator of Peer Tutor Training at the William L. Adams Writing Center at Texas Christian University. He has presented papers at major conferences in the field, including NCTE, the National Writing Centers Association Conference, the North American Interdisciplinary Wilderness Conference, and the Rocky Mountain MLA Conference and has read his fiction at the Conference of College Teachers of English, the Arkansas Philological Association, and the Fort Concho Museum Literary Festival. He is co-editor of *Descant*, TCU's creative writing journal. He has published essays in *Writing Lab Newsletter*, *The Writing Center Journal*, *Northern Lights*, *Outside*, *Weber Studies*, and *English in Texas*; his fiction has appeared in *New Texas Voices '92*. With Christina Murphy, he is the author of *The St. Martin's Sourcebook for Writing Tutors*.

Jeanne Simpson is a professor of English and Assistant Vice President for Academic Affairs at Eastern Illinois University. She earned her B.A. from Texas Tech University, her M.A. from the University of Texas at Austin, and her Doctor of Arts degree in rhetoric and composition from Illinois State University. She established Eastern's writing center in 1981 and directed it for nine years. She was a founding member of the National Writing Centers Association and served as its third president. With Ray Wallace, she co-edited *The Writing Center: New Directions* (Garland, 1991).

Mark Waldo is Director of the Writing Center and Associate Professor of English at the University of Nevada. His research interests include the relationship between writing centers and WAC, writing assessment, and Romantic rhetoric; his most recent publications in those areas have appeared in *Writing Program Administrator*, *The Writing Center Journal*, and *Halcyon: A Journal for the Humanities*. He is currently writing a book on writing centers and discipline-based WAC.

Mary Webb teaches composition, technical writing, and literature at the University of Nevada, Reno. She has written a book about the environment and water use in western Nevada, forthcoming from the University of Nevada Press. She has presented several papers at writing across the curriculum and writing center conferences; she works in the University of Nevada Writing Center with faculty from electrical engineering, assessing writing among engineering students.

Jennifer Welsh is a graduate student in the Rhetoric, Linguistics, and Literature Program in the English Department at the University of Southern California. She teaches writing at USC and at Pepperdine University.

Carmen Werder is Associate Director of the University Writing Programs at Western Washington University, where she oversees the daily operations of the Writing Center, consults with faculty in writing across the disciplines, and teaches a writing course linked with the social sciences as part of a learning community cluster. She has taught beginning, intermediate, and advanced writing courses and also served as Assistant Director of Composition, 1989-90. One of her essays in the *Minnesota English Journal* (1986) won an award for best article.